™

References for the Rest of Us!™

BESTSELLING BOOK SERIES

Do you find that traditional reference books are overloaded with technical details and advice you'll never use? Do you postpone important life decisions because you just don't want to deal with them? Then our *...For Dummies*® business and general reference book series is for you.

...For Dummies business and general reference books are written for those frustrated and hard-working souls who know they aren't dumb, but find that the myriad of personal and business issues and the accompanying horror stories make them feel helpless. *...For Dummies* books use a lighthearted approach, a down-to-earth style, and even cartoons and humorous icons to dispel fears and build confidence. Lighthearted but not lightweight, these books are perfect survival guides to solve your everyday personal and business problems.

> *"More than a publishing phenomenon, 'Dummies' is a sign of the times."*
>
> — The New York Times

> *"A world of detailed and authoritative information is packed into them..."*
>
> — U.S. News and World Report

> *"...you won't go wrong buying them."*
>
> — Walter Mossberg, Wall Street Journal, on IDG Books' ...For Dummies books

Already, millions of satisfied readers agree. They have made *...For Dummies* the #1 introductory level computer book series and a best-selling business book series. They have written asking for more. So, if you're looking for the best and easiest way to learn about business and other general reference topics, look to *...For Dummies* to give you a helping hand.

IDG
BOOKS
WORLDWIDE

1/99

Coaching Kids FOR DUMMIES®

by Rick Wolff

IDG Books Worldwide, Inc.
An International Data Group Company

Foster City, CA ◆ Chicago, IL ◆ Indianapolis, IN ◆ New York, NY

Coaching Kids For Dummies®

Published by
IDG Books Worldwide, Inc.
An International Data Group Company
919 E. Hillsdale Blvd.
Suite 400
Foster City, CA 94404
www.idgbooks.com (IDG Books Worldwide Web site)
www.dummies.com (Dummies Press Web site)

Library of Congress Catalog Card No.: 99-69702

ISBN: 0-7645-5197-3

Printed in the United States of America

10 9 8 7 6 5 4 3 2 1

1O/QX/QT/QQ/IN

Distributed in the United States by IDG Books Worldwide, Inc.

Distributed by CDG Books Canada Inc. for Canada; by Transworld Publishers Limited in the United Kingdom; by IDG Norge Books for Norway; by IDG Sweden Books for Sweden; by IDG Books Australia Publishing Corporation Pty. Ltd. for Australia and New Zealand; by TransQuest Publishers Pte Ltd. for Singapore, Malaysia, Thailand, Indonesia, and Hong Kong; by Gotop Information Inc. for Taiwan; by ICG Muse, Inc. for Japan; by Intersoft for South Africa; by Eyrolles for France; by International Thomson Publishing for Germany, Austria and Switzerland; by Distribuidora Cuspide for Argentina; by LR International for Brazil; by Galileo Libros for Chile; by Ediciones ZETA S.C.R. Ltda. for Peru; by WS Computer Publishing Corporation, Inc., for the Philippines; by Contemporanea de Ediciones for Venezuela; by Express Computer Distributors for the Caribbean and West Indies; by Micronesia Media Distributor, Inc. for Micronesia; by Chips Computadoras S.A. de C.V. for Mexico; by Editorial Norma de Panama S.A. for Panama; by American Bookshops for Finland.

For general information on IDG Books Worldwide's books in the U.S., please call our Consumer Customer Service department at 800-762-2974. For reseller information, including discounts and premium sales, please call our Reseller Customer Service department at 800-434-3422.

For information on where to purchase IDG Books Worldwide's books outside the U.S., please contact our International Sales department at 317-596-5530 or fax 317-572-4002.

For consumer information on foreign language translations, please contact our Customer Service department at 1-800-434-3422, fax 317-572-4002, or e-mail rights@idgbooks.com.

For information on licensing foreign or domestic rights, please phone +1-650-653-7098.

For sales inquiries and special prices for bulk quantities, please contact our Order Services department at 800-434-3422 or write to the address above.

For information on using IDG Books Worldwide's books in the classroom or for ordering examination copies, please contact our Educational Sales department at 800-434-2086 or fax 317-572-4005.

For press review copies, author interviews, or other publicity information, please contact our Public Relations department at 650-653-7000 or fax 650-653-7500.

For authorization to photocopy items for corporate, personal, or educational use, please contact Copyright Clearance Center, 222 Rosewood Drive, Danvers, MA 01923, or fax 978-750-4470.

About the Author

Rick Wolff is a nationally-recognized expert in the field of sports psychology and performance enhancement. Often quoted by the media about the issues that face today's athletes, Rick has written and lectured widely on the psychological pressures that accompany America's passion for sports.

A former professional baseball player in the Detroit Tigers' organization, Rick also served as the roving sports psychology coach for the Cleveland Indians from 1990 to 1994. He's worked with dozens of top professional and collegiate athletes, including players from the National Football League, the National Hockey League, and Major League Baseball. Before joining the Indians, Rick was the head baseball coach at Mercy College (New York) for eight years, where his teams were nationally ranked in NCAA Division II.

Rich is one of the founders and serves as the chairman of The Center for Sports Parenting, which is part of the Institute for International Sport. He hosts a weekly sports parenting program ("The Sports Edge") on WFAN Radio in New York City. He's been featured on ESPN, the Madison Square Garden Network, SportsChannel, *The Today Show, Good Morning America, 20/20, CBS This Morning,* CNBC, A&E, PBS, Lifetime, and dozens of other outlets. In 1997, Rick co-hosted an original videotape program, *YOUTH SPORTS,* with Steve Young, the All-Pro quarterback with the San Francisco 49ers.

Rick's byline has appeared in such well-known publications as *Sports Illustrated, SI for Kids, The New York Times, USA Today, GQ, Harvard Magazine, Sesame Street Magazine, Child, Scholastic, Family Life, Psychology Today, Readers' Digest,* and many others.

Rick graduated magna cum laude in psychology from Harvard University and with high honors in psychology in his graduate studies at Long Island University. He's a longtime member of the Association for the Advancement of Applied Sports Psychology and as well as the American Baseball Coaches Association.

Rick and his wife, Trish, have three children — John, Alyssa, and Samantha. They reside in Armonk, New York.

ABOUT IDG BOOKS WORLDWIDE

Welcome to the world of IDG Books Worldwide.

IDG Books Worldwide, Inc., is a subsidiary of International Data Group, the world's largest publisher of computer-related information and the leading global provider of information services on information technology. IDG was founded more than 30 years ago by Patrick J. McGovern and now employs more than 9,000 people worldwide. IDG publishes more than 290 computer publications in over 75 countries. More than 90 million people read one or more IDG publications each month.

Launched in 1990, IDG Books Worldwide is today the #1 publisher of best-selling computer books in the United States. We are proud to have received eight awards from the Computer Press Association in recognition of editorial excellence and three from Computer Currents' First Annual Readers' Choice Awards. Our best-selling *...For Dummies*® series has more than 50 million copies in print with translations in 31 languages. IDG Books Worldwide, through a joint venture with IDG's Hi-Tech Beijing, became the first U.S. publisher to publish a computer book in the People's Republic of China. In record time, IDG Books Worldwide has become the first choice for millions of readers around the world who want to learn how to better manage their businesses.

Our mission is simple: Every one of our books is designed to bring extra value and skill-building instructions to the reader. Our books are written by experts who understand and care about our readers. The knowledge base of our editorial staff comes from years of experience in publishing, education, and journalism — experience we use to produce books to carry us into the new millennium. In short, we care about books, so we attract the best people. We devote special attention to details such as audience, interior design, use of icons, and illustrations. And because we use an efficient process of authoring, editing, and desktop publishing our books electronically, we can spend more time ensuring superior content and less time on the technicalities of making books.

You can count on our commitment to deliver high-quality books at competitive prices on topics you want to read about. At IDG Books Worldwide, we continue in the IDG tradition of delivering quality for more than 30 years. You'll find no better book on a subject than one from IDG Books Worldwide.

John Kilcullen

John Kilcullen
Chairman and CEO
IDG Books Worldwide, Inc.

Eighth Annual
Computer Press
Awards ≥ 1992

Ninth Annual
Computer Press
Awards ≥ 1993

Tenth Annual
Computer Press
Awards ≥ 1994

Eleventh Annual
Computer Press
Awards ≥ 1995

IDG is the world's leading IT media, research and exposition company. Founded in 1964, IDG had 1997 revenues of $2.05 billion and has more than 9,000 employees worldwide. IDG offers the widest range of media options that reach IT buyers in 75 countries representing 95% of worldwide IT spending. IDG's diverse product and services portfolio spans six key areas including print publishing, online publishing, expositions and conferences, market research, education and training, and global marketing services. More than 90 million people read one or more of IDG's 290 magazines and newspapers, including IDG's leading global brands — Computerworld, PC World, Network World, Macworld and the Channel World family of publications. IDG Books Worldwide is one of the fastest-growing computer book publishers in the world, with more than 700 titles in 36 languages. The "...For Dummies®" series alone has more than 50 million copies in print. IDG offers online users the largest network of technology-specific Web sites around the world through IDG.net (http://www.idg.net), which comprises more than 225 targeted Web sites in 55 countries worldwide. International Data Corporation (IDC) is the world's largest provider of information technology data, analysis and consulting, with research centers in over 41 countries and more than 400 research analysts worldwide. IDG World Expo is a leading producer of more than 168 globally branded conferences and expositions in 35 countries including E3 (Electronic Entertainment Expo), Macworld Expo, ComNet, Windows World Expo, ICE (Internet Commerce Expo), Agenda, DEMO, and Spotlight. IDG's training subsidiary, ExecuTrain, is the world's largest computer training company, with more than 230 locations worldwide and 785 training courses. IDG Marketing Services helps industry-leading IT companies build international brand recognition by developing global integrated marketing programs via IDG's print, online and exposition products worldwide. Further information about the company can be found at www.idg.com. 1/26/00

Author's Acknowledgments

I know first-hand what a challenging task it can be to publish a sports title in a timely fashion. And to that end, I want to personally thank those key people who, along the way, have made this project a most enjoyable one.

The project began at IDG with my editor, Stacy Collins, who's a true joy to work with. Her colleagues, Lisa Roule, Pam Mourouzis, and Janet Withers, are terrific professionals as well. I also want to offer a special thanks to Tere Drenth, who was assigned to this project late in the race, but kicked in down the stretch in a big way.

I want to thank my colleague Bob Bigelow for helping in the review of the materials. I just wished more parents and coaches shared the same kind of passion that Bob has regarding the right way to work with kids in sports.

My sincere thanks to my trusty editorial colleague, Dan Ambrosio. Despite his being a Phillies fan, his efforts on my behalf are sincerely appreciated.

Finally, and most importantly, I'd like to thank my wonderful wife, Trish, and our children, John, Alyssa, and Samantha, for teaching me along the way about coaching kids. Few activities in life are as spiritually rewarding as watching one's children have fun while playing sports.

Publisher's Acknowledgments

We're proud of this book; please register your comments through our IDG Books Worldwide Online Registration Form located at http://my2cents.dummies.com.

Some of the people who helped bring this book to market include the following:

Acquisitions and Editorial

Project Editors: Tere Drenth, Pamela Mourouzis

Acquisitions Editor: Stacy S. Collins

General Reviewer: Bob Bigelow

Copy Editor: Janet M. Withers

Editorial Coordinator: Lisa Roule

Editorial Director: Kristin A. Cocks

Production

Project Coordinator: Shawn Aylsworth

Layout and Graphics: Amy Adrian, Barry Offringa, Tracy K. Oliver, Jill Piscitelli, Brent Savage, Brian Torwelle, Dan Whetstine, Erin Zeltner

Proofreaders: Laura Albert, Corey Bowen, John Greenough, Marianne Santy, Charles Spencer

Indexer: Liz Cunningham

Special Help
Amanda Foxworth Michelle Hacker, Kristin Nash, Kevin Thornton

---

General and Administrative

IDG Books Worldwide, Inc.: John Kilcullen, CEO

IDG Books Technology Publishing Group: Richard Swadley, Senior Vice President and Publisher; Walter Bruce III, Vice President and Associate Publisher; Joseph Wikert, Associate Publisher; Mary Bednarek, Branded Product Development Director; Mary Corder, Editorial Director; Barry Pruett, Publishing Manager; Michelle Baxter, Publishing Manager

IDG Books Consumer Publishing Group: Roland Elgey, Senior Vice President and Publisher; Kathleen A. Welton, Vice President and Publisher; Kevin Thornton, Acquisitions Manager; Kristin A. Cocks, Editorial Director

IDG Books Internet Publishing Group: Brenda McLaughlin, Senior Vice President and Publisher; Diane Graves Steele, Vice President and Associate Publisher; Sofia Marchant, Online Marketing Manager

IDG Books Production for Dummies Press: Debbie Stailey, Associate Director of Production; Cindy L. Phipps, Manager of Project Coordination, Production Proofreading, and Indexing; Tony Augsburger, Manager of Prepress, Reprints, and Systems; Laura Carpenter, Production Control Manager; Shelley Lea, Supervisor of Graphics and Design; Debbie J. Gates, Production Systems Specialist; Robert Springer, Supervisor of Proofreading; Kathie Schutte, Production Supervisor

Dummies Packaging and Book Design: Patty Page, Manager, Promotions Marketing

◆

The publisher would like to give special thanks to Patrick J. McGovern, without whom this book would not have been possible.

◆

Contents at a Glance

Cartoons at a Glance

By Rich Tennant

page 7

page 71

page 141

page 119

page 179

Fax: 978-546-7747
E-mail: richtennant@the5thwave.com
World Wide Web: www.the5thwave.com

Table of Contents

· ·

Introduction

● ●

*W*hat could be easier — and more fun — than coaching kids in youth sports? After all, how complicated can this challenge be? It's about fun and games — and that should be simple, right?

Sadly, coaching kids isn't that simple. Any Mom or Dad who has ever watched a youth league sports game knows that all sorts of pressures, worries, concerns, and emotions are involved when your son or daughter is out there competing. In fact, it's the rare parent today who hasn't witnessed at least one ugly incident at a youth league game where either a coach or a parent has gotten out of control. And if anything, this problem has only become worse in recent years, and there's no indication that it's going to improve any time soon.

But there is some good news here, and it all starts with you. As a coach yourself, you have a terrific opportunity to make certain that kids do have fun, that their physical and psychological needs are met, and that they all come away having enjoyed the experience of playing for you and wanting to play on your team again next year. That's what this book is centered on — how you can become the very best coach you can be, no matter what sport you coach.

About This Book

This book is designed for the parent or teacher who has never coached before, but who would like to join in the fun. It's deliberately written to be useful for all coaches, no matter what sport they're involved in. Regardless of the sport or the age of the kids — whether they're just starting out at age 5 or 6 or are as old as 13 or 14 — youth coaches face a variety of universal coaching situations at one time or another:

- ✔ What do you say to your kids after they've just lost a close game?
- ✔ How do you handle an angry parent who feels that his or her child isn't getting enough quality playing time?
- ✔ How do you motivate the kid who doesn't pay attention in practice?

These are just a few of the kinds of commonplace minor crises that youth coaches invariably run into each season. This book covers these — and a whole lot more, providing tips, insights, statistics, and practical dialogues that you can adapt to typical coaching situations. Throughout, you can find all sorts of charts and coaching tools that you can readily adapt to help you organize each practice and prepare for each game.

Whether you read this book from cover to cover or turn to the chapter that fills an immediate need, it has been developed specifically to give you quick and practical answers.

Foolish Assumptions

In *Coaching Kids For Dummies,* I assume that you have the following priorities for the kids who sign up for your team:

- ✔ You want the kids to have fun.
- ✔ You want them to become physically fit.
- ✔ You want to develop a sense of team camaraderie.
- ✔ You want the kids to develop some athletic skills along the way.

These assumptions are important, because there are certain things that this book isn't about. It isn't, for example, intended to give you inside secrets on how to ensure that your team will win the league championship or that individual youngsters will develop into potential professional athletes. While competition is a vital and important aspect of all sports, the bullets listed above are the primary focus of these pages.

In addition, I assume that you already have some sense of the sport you're going to coach: If you're going to coach a soccer team, you've seen a soccer game at one point or another in your life and are working toward a basic understanding of the rules of the game (for example, that only the goalkeeper can handle the ball with his hands). A variety of *...For Dummies* books, including *Football For Dummies, Baseball For Dummies, Soccer For Dummies, Golf For Dummies, Running For Dummies, Skiing For Dummies,* and so on (all published by IDG Books Worldwide, Inc.), can help you master the basics of the sport you're planning to coach.

Finally, I assume that you understand that coaching kids can sometimes put you on the firing line in your town or community. As with any responsibility, coaching a bunch of kids (especially your neighbors' kids) brings along a certain set of expectations from the other parents — and they fully expect you to behave and conduct yourself as a responsible adult. Toward this end, I give you plenty of tips and tricks for managing the public relations side of coaching kids.

How This Book Is Organized

The overall organization of the book is designed for easy access for every youth coach — and for parents as well. It makes no difference which age bracket of kids or which sport you're coaching, simply flip to the parts and chapters that are most applicable to your situation.

Part I: A Parent's Primer

This part starts with a basic overview of youth sports competition that every coach (and parent) should read. It goes into detail as to how young children first become attracted to playing sports and how they develop a sense of self-esteem from mastering certain athletic skills. I've also included a discussion of the right age to first introduce your child to organized sports, and what kind of expectations you should have (or not have) for your child. Finally, I include a chapter that takes apart the mythology of travel teams — a chapter that all sports coaches and parents should read.

Part II: Coaching Tasks

In this part, I include a complete analysis of what you need to know to prepare for every practice and game. I explain in detail how to set up each practice session on a minute-by-minute basis, what you have to do for each game day, how to set up that all-important first team meeting with the kids and their parents, and of course, how to actually coach a bunch of excited youngsters during a game. This part deals with the essence of coaching youth sports.

Part III: Motivation and the Mental Game

This part deals specifically with communication and motivational skills that every coach needs to know when dealing with today's youth. Remember, what may have motivated you when you were a kid playing sports may not work for kids playing sports in the 21st century — kids today may expect different methods of motivation when competing. This part helps you figure what works — and what doesn't.

Part IV: Coaching Challenges

Part IV focuses on those all too common (but most challenging) aspects of coaching: dealing with concerns about playing time, handling hostile parents, coaching your own child, interacting with injured players, and understanding the stresses of the job. Experienced youth coaches say that the Xs and Os of coaching are the easy part, while working with angry moms and dads, injured players, and your own children causes many new coaches to lose enthusiasm for the job. Knowing how to react in these difficult situations is vital for every youth coach.

Part V: The Part of Tens

Part V is the Part of Tens, specializing in pointers for parents, providing hot tips for coaching kids, and giving resources for coaches everywhere. These serve as a quick round-up or review of the topics covered in more detail throughout the book.

Appendixes

Appendix A contains a listing of the most common and well-known youth sports organizations throughout North America, including addresses, phone numbers, and other basic information.

Appendix B is a coach's resource kit: a potpourri of everything you need before you head out to practice or the game.

Icons Used in This Book

Throughout this book, you can find little pictures — called *icons* — in the margins of nearly every page. These icons direct your attention to information that is especially relevant for you. Here's what they all mean:

Tips, tricks, pointers, and techniques that all coaches should keep in mind.

Real-life or made-up examples of situations, conversations, and suggested scripts for concerned parents and coaches.

Interesting tidbits of information about kids and sports.

Ideas to keep in mind for future reference.

Fore! Incoming! These icons alert you to potentially challenging situations.

Where to Go from Here

You can get into this book in a number of ways: You can read it cover-to-cover or start with any chapter of the book and flip to other chapters as needed. Or, if you want to look up a specific problem in the index and just read a paragraph or two, that's fine as well.

Of interest to a lot of coaches and parents is Chapter 4, which discusses the pros and cons of travel teams. You may also want to check out Chapters 7 and 8, which give you tips and tricks for organizing your team's practices. You may also want to take a peek at Chapter 15, which deals with the unique stresses of being a youth coach in your town or community. As any experienced youth coach will tell you, a lot of emotion goes into working with youngsters and their parents, and as a new coach, you'll be well served if you're prepared for it.

Part I
A Parent's Primer

"Someone's got to break it to Mr. Swanzy that his son is just too young to play third base."

In this part . . .

*1*n this part, you find out about both good — and not-so-good — aspects of youth sports. Because coaching kids in sports tends to be such an emotionally-charged issue for parents and coaches, you get a brief overview of how kids are first introduced to youth sports and what you, as a parent or coach, must be aware of before sending your child off to play on a team. Along the way, you find out about highly competitive travel teams, individual versus team sports, and the proper age for your youngster to get involved.

Chapter 1

An Introduction to Sports Parenting

> *"The best thing about Little League baseball is that it gives the parents something to do on the weekends and keeps them off the streets."*
>
> — An anonymous (yet wise) sports parent

*W*elcome to the magical world of sports parenting. For many sports-loving parents and children, these years are filled with wonderful memories, exciting moments, and dreams of future athletic glory. The vast majority of kids who register and play organized youth sports have a terrific time. And the parents who volunteer to give their time as coaches, assistant coaches, or team parents share in the smiles and joy of the children.

However, problems or concerns can crop up. And curiously, these days, in which sports have truly become the universal language no matter where you go in your travels, there really aren't any clear roadmaps or textbooks for parents who want to get involved at the youth sports level.

The purpose of this chapter (and the rest of the chapters in this part) is precisely that — to fill in the gap of helping parents become the very best sports parents they can be, and in doing so, to help ensure that each child on their team thoroughly enjoys the experience.

Getting Started

The following are the kinds of comments that youth league coaches tend to hear from parents:

- ✔ "I'm convinced that my son is on the absolute right track to become a Major-League pitcher, and I want to know what good baseball summer camps you recommend for talented 9-year-olds."

- ✔ "Lots of people have told us that Sheila is definitely going to be a star figure skater. Shouldn't we be looking for a special skating coach for her? She's only 7, but after all, the clock is ticking."

- ✔ "What kinds of exercises and drills should my little guy be doing? He doesn't start organized soccer until he's 5, but I want him to be ready and in top form right from the start."

- ✔ "Look, my child has a very busy schedule — she has piano lessons, rehearsals for the school play, religious instruction, and some occasional tutoring. So, she's not going to be able to make many of the practice sessions, but we still expect her to get a good amount of playing time in the games. That isn't a problem for you, is it, Coach?"

These questions are typical of the kinds of concerns that parents everywhere express on a routine basis. The best way for you as a coach to answer these questions is to ask a more basic and fundamental question:

"What do you want your child to get out of sports?"

Sounds like a fairly straightforward question, doesn't it? But for many parents, this question is a little more difficult to answer than you may think. After all, lots of moms and dads are certain that their children will be offered college athletic scholarships to play sports (see "The odds of getting that free ride" sidebar). Other parents daydream about their sons playing in the big leagues and making millions, or their daughters thrilling international crowds with her moves on the ice and winning the gold medal in the Olympics. And lots of others merely want their children to experience the joy of being a member of a sports team, to have a chance to exercise, and to develop a passion for a sport (or sports) that may last a lifetime.

KID FACT

The odds of getting that free ride

According to the National Center for Educational Statistics, less than one percent of all the kids playing organized sports today will ever qualify for a college athletic scholarship. (Source: *Time,* July 12, 1999)

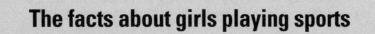

The facts about girls playing sports

Does it make sense for girls to get involved in sports? Consider the following:

✔ Recent research findings indicate that many high school female athletes report higher grades and higher marks on standardized test scores, and are more likely to go on to college than their non-athletic counterparts.

✔ Eighty percent of the women identified as key leaders in *Fortune* 500 companies participated in sports during their childhood.

✔ Girls now comprise about 37 percent of all high school athletes. That represents a substantial increase from the 1 in 27 girls who participated in sports in 1971 to 1 in 3 girls now. And the numbers continue to go up.

✔ Playing sports pays off in lots of positive medical ways for girls: reduction of symptoms of stress and depression, a reduced risk of obesity and coronary heart disease, and a reduced risk of osteoporosis. Participation in sports also enhances their sense of self-esteem and self-confidence.

(Source: The President's Council on Physical Fitness and Sports Report)

Becoming an effective sports parent means thoughtfully evaluating what you want your child to take away from the youth sports experience. Your decision has a major bearing on your philosophy of how your child interacts with the ever-expanding world of youth sports.

Chances are, you know the odds of your child ever playing pro ball or getting to the Olympics. As an adult, you know intellectually that the odds are truly stacked against your or any other child becoming the next Michael Jordan or Tara Lipinski. In fact, statistically speaking, your child has a much better chance of becoming a physician, attorney, or company CEO than of getting paid a thin dime for doing something athletic.

Is this to suggest that, because the odds are stacked against your child playing in the NFL or the WNBA, he or she may as well give up? No, of course not. Rather, the goal — especially for those parents whose children are just starting out in sports — is to keep sports in perspective. Understand that first and foremost, kids play sports for the following reasons:

✔ It's fun.

✔ They enjoy being with their classmates.

✔ They enjoy wearing new uniforms.

✔ They get some fresh air and exercise their bodies.

It was the great Hall of Fame coach (and Greek philosopher) Plato who first talked about "a sound body and a sound mind." That's still excellent advice, even in the 21st century. If your little ones can find a passion for a sport — any sport — chances are good that they will continue to play that sport as they get older, even beyond high school and into their adult years. And by the way, this advice applies equally to both boys and girls.

Girls who play sports as youngsters grow up to be healthier women, have a better sense of self-esteem, and are less likely to become pregnant at an early age (see "The facts about girls playing sports" sidebar). Beyond that, girls (just like boys) find that playing sports is a wonderful social experience in terms of making friendships, enjoying team camaraderie, and aspiring toward goals — besides, they have a lot of fun as well.

Soccer Moms Register Here!

The popular phrase of the 1990s, "soccer mom," described the hectic life-style of the "on-the-go" mother. The phrase captures the essence of shuffling children from one youth sports event to another.

Being a sports parent today is rarely a casual experience, for either the child or the parent. Along the way, you have to deal with

✔ Registration and uniforms ("Is my 8-year-old a youth large or an adult small?")

✔ Time management for practice sessions ("I work on Saturday mornings, and so does my husband . . . can't you schedule the practices for some other time?") and games ("It looks like rain. Is the game cancelled for today?")

✔ Coaches with behavioral problems ("Coach, how dare you use that kind of language around my child!")

✔ Insensitive neighbors ("My 9-year-old is such a star! In fact, she's being recruited for several travel teams.")

✔ Kids who aren't always that interested in playing the sport ("Mom, can't I stay here this morning and just watch television?")

And if you have more than one child playing sports, you have to juggle your schedule in order to accommodate everybody's situation. For many parents, youth sports consumes a good chunk of the weekends from Labor Day in September right through the end of the school year. In many cases, children are involved in youth sports programs that last all year.

Your investment in your child's sport — the time and energy you spend taking your child to practices, raising money, attending games or meets, and so on — may seem all the more frustrating if your child doesn't display true promise. But you don't do all of this so that your child can get a college scholarship; you do it to let her have fun, enjoy herself, and feel good about her efforts.

The key to sports greatness: passion

If you listen to great athletes talk about their careers, invariably they have one theme in common: a singular passion for their sport. That passion drove them to great heights. They didn't succeed just to please a parent or a coach.

Michael Jordan and Wayne Gretzky, who dominated their respective sports of basketball and ice hockey, often talk about their competitive drive as well as their enjoyment of their games. And as every schoolchild in America can gladly tell you, Jordan not only wasn't a star basketball player when he was a freshman in high school, but he didn't make his high school team even as a sophomore!

It wasn't because he had an "attitude problem" or some other behavioral concern that his coach didn't like. Rather, Jordan just wasn't as good as the other kids on the team. But rather than turn his back on basketball, he decided as a 15-year-old on two things:

- He really loved playing the game.

- He was going to do everything he could to make the team the following year.

That he did, and within a few short years, he went from being just another kid in North Carolina who couldn't make his varsity team to becoming the premier player in the country.

Wayne Gretzky, on the other hand, always was a star when growing up in Canada. He scored goals and assists in record-setting fashion. But even when he was 18 years old and headed to the National Hockey League, plenty of people doubted Gretzky's abilities. In the rough-and-tumble world of pro hockey, there was considerable concern as to how the 5-11, 160-pound Gretzky would be able to survive the fierce body checking of the NHL.

Even worse, whenever the Edmonton Oilers — Gretzky's pro team — did physical exams in training camp, Gretzky was rated as last in physical strength, reflexes, foot speed, and vision. The odds were certainly against him having much of a splash in the NHL. But no matter. Because of his love of the sport and his competitive drive, Gretzky went out that season and set a National Hockey League single season scoring record. When Wayne finally retired from hockey in 1999, he kept saying in his retirement press conference how much he loved playing the game.

Some basic parental common sense goes a long way when parenting kids in sports, and keeping sports in perspective is vital for both you and your children. Don't worry so much about whether they're scoring all the goals or making the All-Star team. Instead, focus your attention on whether they're enjoying the experience.

As a parent, your job is to gently remind your children that although it's nice to aim for a career in sports, they should think about other career dreams as well. Grant Hill, the NBA superstar, remembers that when he was growing up in suburban Virginia, his parents always reminded him to have two parachutes in life, just as paratroopers always pack two chutes with them when they jump, Grant's parents made clear that it was okay for Grant to chase a sports career, but he also had to have another career plan — a backup parachute — in case that first dream didn't become reality.

Talk to your children about their dreams, and rather than limiting them to only one, encourage them to explore different career possibilities. Mention the following examples to your youngsters when they're just starting out in sports, and get them thinking early on about packing two parachutes.

- ✔ Brian MacRae, a major league outfielder, also works as a radio personality when he's not playing ball.

- ✔ Cheryl Miller, the former college basketball star, has worked both as a coach and a sportscaster since she finished playing ball.

- ✔ George Medich, who pitched for several years in the majors, went to medical school in the off-season. So did Dot Richardson, the star shortstop of the 1998 U.S. Olympic women's softball team.

- ✔ Tim Green, the former NFL star for the Atlanta Falcons, finished law school in his off-time. So did Steve Young of the San Francisco 49ers.

Back When I Was a Kid . . .

Your approach to your child's sports career may have something to do with your perception of how good you were in sports as a kid. Be honest with yourself: Were you just a casual athlete? Did you play on the high school varsity? In college? Were you a star? Or just another kid on the team? (Be as objective as you possibly can, because your memory of your sports career can have a major influence on how you view your child's sporting experience.) This section can help you better understand your motivations.

Gauging just how successful your own youth sports career was should be easy — it's over. You may have lots of reasons why you never played center field for the Yankees ("I had a string of bad coaches" or "My eyes aren't that good" or "If only I hadn't quit the high school team"), but except for a very small percentage of parents, most moms and dads never get beyond high school sports as an active athlete. And a significant portion of today's sports parents didn't play many sports as kids at all.

There's nothing wrong with any of this, but bear in mind that a parent's wistful wishes about his own childhood sports dreams may have an undue influence on how he raises his kids. Although it's fine to encourage your child to pursue her best efforts in sports, always bear in mind that the little person out there competing is *not* you — but a little person who is merely related to you. There's a big difference.

Fondly remembering the old days

There was a time, perhaps 30 or 40 years ago, that the term "sports parent" wasn't well known. In fact, back in the 1950s and 1960s, the only time anyone observed a sports parent was when someone noticed that a pushy father with athletic aspirations for his son was being too hard on his kid — that he was "living vicariously" through his son. This image conjures up a number of famous American sports movies, such as *The Bad News Bears* and *Fear Strikes Out,* in which out-of-control dads with unrealistic expectations put too much pressure on their athletically oriented kids.

These days, the parents who are involved with youth sports are much calmer, much more relaxed, and much more supportive of kids just having fun . . . right? Of course not. If anything, thanks to the increased popularity of sports over the last two decades, parents are more involved than ever before in their kids' athletic development — and that includes both boys and girls sports, starting at age 5 (and often even younger than that).

No matter what town, community, or neighborhood you go to in North America today, you can find some sort of organized youth sports program. Some are organized by local recreational departments, some by parents, and some by local religious organizations, but whether you're in a small coastal town in Maine or in the desert climate of Phoenix, you find youth sports everywhere. And wherever I go, especially when I address community or recreational groups, I'm always told, "You know, in this town, we take our youth sports very seriously."

In the 1950s and 1960s, life — especially when it involved youth sports — was measurably simpler. Little League baseball, which was started in 1939 and gained popularity in the 1940s, was still beginning to grow. Other national organizations, such as Pop Warner football and Catholic Youth Organization basketball, were also just beginning to gain a following. But for the most part, kids in the 1950s and 1960s (who are now in their 30s, 40s, and 50s, and comprise a good chunk of today's sports parents) were left to their own devices. They learned and played sports on the playgrounds after school, without parents, coaches, umpires, uniforms, or league standings, and with very few of the trappings that routinely accompany organized youth sports today.

Keeping in mind how you started out

Think back for a moment about how you learned to play sports. For many, it was simply a matter of showing up on the ballfield and waiting to be chosen in a pickup game. Traditionally, the two oldest or most talented players chose teams from the kids who wanted to play. From there, the teams would compete, making their own calls without the benefit of an umpire or referee.

If the two teams were somewhat lopsided in terms of the score, invariably the two captains would stop the game, reshuffle the lineups, and then continue the game. (Instinctively, the kids knew that it's more fun to play in a close, competitive game than a game in which one team runs up the score against the other — a lesson that's lost on some parents who coach youth teams today!)

Considering your child's abilities

Fast forward to today. Look at your perception of your child's athletic abilities. Do you think that he's a natural athlete? Or do you think that, with a little work and effort, he could be pretty good? Do you expect him to compete at a higher level — at the high school varsity, college, or professional level?

Lots of parents dream about their children as athletes — that maybe, just maybe, their little one may become that one in a million who signs a multimillion-dollar contract. But the vast majority of parents have to start thinking a little more realistically and perhaps lower their expectations of their little athletic wonder.

 Naturally, you *never* go to your 8-year-old and say, "Son, let's be realistic — chances are you're not going to play for the Green Bay Packers." That's not only wrong, it's poor parenting. Nobody dashed your dreams of playing in the pros when you were a kid, so there's no reason for you to do it to your child. All young athletes have dreams — of seeing themselves making the big hit, scoring the game-winning goal, or just being the star — and that's great. That's a major part of the fun of playing sports.

Gauging whether it's better today

Are organized youth sports better for kids today than the way youth sports used to be? After all, to many parents today, the 1950s and 60s were the golden days of youth sports — a time when kids were left alone to develop their own skills and passions for each sport. But that time has come and gone. Kids today are ushered into sports programs as young as age 4 or 5, and they're forced to understand early on in life that playing sports is not so much about having fun, but mostly about winning and playing up to a parent's or coach's expectations.

Today's young athletes may be bigger, stronger, faster, and more polished than today's sports parents were when they played as kids. But do kids today have as much fun playing sports as their parents did? Sport sociologists keep debating this issue, with no clear-cut answer.

But in much the same way you recognized on your own that you weren't big enough, fast enough, strong enough, or talented enough to keep going in sports, your child may eventually discover this reality of sports as well — but he'll learn this reality on his own terms. That's the key.

Achieving parental balance

In the 1950s, the dad who pushed his kid to higher accomplishments in youth sports was seen as living vicariously through his son. That is, the dad was trying to chase his own athletic glory by pushing the son in sports. Other parents around these fathers criticized such behavior, recognizing the detrimental effects on the child.

These pushy parents really haven't gone away, though. These days, they've simply adapted a new, socially acceptable spin. These parents say that they're not living vicariously through their kids, but rather are simply providing those athletic opportunities to their children that weren't made available to them when they were growing up. Here's an example:

"Sure, I have my child playing on two travel teams at the same time and have hired a personal training coach for him, and I send him away to an exclusive athletic camp each summer for six weeks, but I wouldn't say that I'm pushing him too hard in sports. Nor am I living my sports life through his."

A few years ago, I bumped into a neighbor whose son was totally absorbed in ice hockey. Although the kid was only 9 years old, the proud parent had him playing on travel hockey programs all year round, plus specialized hockey camps all summer. The father couldn't have been happier with his son's progress. I saw the same dad just a few months ago. I asked how his son — who's now 13 — was doing with his ice hockey career. "Well, you know how teenagers are," said the dad wistfully. "He has discovered girls and rock music and the like."

Turns out that the boy is no longer playing ice hockey. He burned out his passion for the game. The sad irony is that as much as the father wanted his son to become a star hockey player, you have to wonder if he unintentionally pushed him too hard and too soon. Burnout is a real concern — more so than ever before in youth sports.

The moral of the story is that you have to maintain a sense of parental balance. Of course you want to see your child succeed in sports, but be careful of pushing her too hard. And especially be careful of pushing her too hard too soon.

What Kids Want . . .

Of all the perceptions, the kids' point of view matters most. After all, the first priority of every youth league is that the kids come first. (And if that isn't the top priority of the league, you may want to reconsider having your child playing in that league!)

. . . From their coaches

The next time you watch your child play in an organized youth sports competition, take a moment and watch the coach instead of watching the action. Most of the time, the coach is exhorting his troops on the field, shouting out encouragement, directions, and suggestions. His voice can usually be heard over the shouting of the other parents in attendance at the game.

Coaches should try to instill a sense of competition, a sense of wanting to do well on the field, and a sense of fair play in the kids on the team. But the most important aspect of coaching a kids' team is to help the children develop a sense of fun and, ideally, a passion to keep playing the sport. Children have plenty of time later on to worry about winning and losing in sports. In the early years, the fundamentals should be emphasized. That's the key to long-range success.

Unfortunately, a number of coaches have great difficulty in maintaining a healthy perspective on youth league sports. They take the team's win-loss record a bit too seriously; they feel that the team's success (or lack thereof) is a direct extension of their ego; or they just don't understand that they're working with young children.

- ✔ Sometimes the coach decides, "Y'know, we have a pretty good team of 8- and 9-year-olds here, and we have a decent chance of winning the league championship." This tempts the coach to play to win at all costs, and that's when problems can arise.

- ✔ Other coaches feel that their responsibility is to instill a strong sense of discipline in their teams, and they become task masters, not unlike army drill sergeants. These coaches develop an overbearing presence that drains all the fun and spontaneity out of the games.

- ✔ Still others are absolutely convinced that the officials are conspiring against their teams. To combat this concern and maintain a psychological edge, these coaches endlessly nag, bother, and annoy the officials throughout the game.

✔ And then there are coaches who see no problem in using profanity around kids. Many times, these coaches say to the team, "Kids, sometimes in the course of a game, I get so involved that I'll occasionally use a bad word or two. Please don't pay attention to the words that I use." This kind of *mea culpa* may be somewhat honorable in intention, but it certainly leaves a bad impression on a child's tender ears.

On a soccer team of 4th and 5th graders, Coach Mike decided that if he gave the majority of the playing time to five of his more-talented athletes, the team would have a better chance of winning the league championship. He also made certain that those five kids played the most desirable positions.

Sure enough, the team won most of its games and went on to win the championship in the local rec league. But at the end-of-the-year team party, Coach Mike was stunned when he found that most of the kids didn't particularly enjoy the experience. "C'mon, what's wrong with you guys?" Coach Mike asked. "We won the league championship, didn't we?"

"But we didn't care about the stupid championship," one of the 10-year-olds who sat on the bench piped up. "We just wanted to play and have fun — all of us!"

This blind spot is the kind of lack of perspective that a youth coach can suffer from. A few years ago, one significant study found that more than 90 percent of the kids asked said that they would prefer to play on a losing team (and play a lot) than sit on the bench and play sparingly on a winning team. (Source: T. Orlick; *Canadian Association for Health, Physical Education, and Recreation Journal,* Sept/Oct 1974)

Watch out for travel team coaches!

The coaches of travel teams can be severe. With travel teams, unlike local recreational programs, coaches often feel that they have a mandate to win at all costs and that they're empowered to try any coaching approach that they feel is suitable for the team or individual player.

Hence, such coaches don't have a problem with sitting out a kid for an entire game ("Look, we played a very tough opponent today, and your child wouldn't have helped our team effort"), playing a child in a less-than-preferred position ("Yes, I know that Sally wants to play forward, but your daughter is better suited to playing fullback"), or verbally chewing out a team or player for not getting the job done on the field ("Mark, if you aren't going to make that play, we're going to have to find someone on this team who can").

For more detail regarding travel teams, flip to Chapter 4.

As a coach and/or parent, take a moment to understand what that survey really says: For kids, the fun is in the playing. Young kids also tend to work from the premise that if they play more on a losing team, their team's chances for winning improve. Likewise, the survey also suggests that kids don't get much of a thrill having to sit on the bench and applaud the athletic heroics of their teammates.

Those two realities should always be at the root of every coach's game plan. The fun is in the playing. And playing a lot.

If, as a youth coach, you find that you have difficulty separating your sense of winning at all costs from allowing all the kids to play, you should rethink your involvement as a youth coach. Remember, it's not about your ego or your personal win-loss record. It's about the kids who have signed up to be on the team, and who harbor their own dreams of thrills, excitement, and fun.

And Mom and Dad — if you think that your child's coach isn't maintaining this perspective, it's your right to approach the coach about your concerns. However, that doesn't mean getting in the coach's face before, during, or after the game. It means taking a civil and mature approach to the situation, and discussing the matter with the coach over the phone or in person, away from the game (perhaps a day or two later). Cooperation is the key: Never be confrontational. This is the only effective way of communicating your concerns to the coach.

. . . From their parents

The biggest difference between kids and parents and their view of sports is that parents have a "finite" view of the game and their child's progress. That's in direct contrast to the kids' perspective, who see today's game as nothing more than one more game in a long chain of games that they are going to play over the length of their childhood.

In other words, many parents, realizing that the time span of playing sports is fairly short, often wonder to themselves: "Is Joey doing well for his age bracket?" or "Sarah hasn't scored a goal in weeks — maybe she's falling behind the others" or "I'm worried about Eric — he doesn't seem to be as aggressive as the other kids on the team."

In these instances, the parents are worrying that their 8- or 10-year-old is falling behind the curve of competitive athletics. Nobody has ever defined what "falling behind the curve" means, but it's assumed that the child somehow has fallen from the ranks of being one of the more talented athletes to being just one of the average masses. For many parents, this fate seems worse than death.

KID FACT

Top ten things parents don't get about kids and sports

Mom and Dad, you may think you know everything about kids and sports, but according to *SI For Kids* magazine, you may be surprised to find out the following:

✔ During the car ride to the game or practice, don't feel compelled to teach kids how to do this or that during the game. Says one 12-year-old about this kind of last-minute parental instruction: "I am not stupid. I know how to play the game."

✔ Kids don't need parental help in getting "psyched up" for the game. They do it themselves.

✔ During the game, be careful not to miss the games or to be too busy chatting with your friends. Kids hate it when you miss their big plays.

✔ If you don't know the strategies of the sport, don't be so eager to offer coaching advice during the game.

✔ Even if you do know the strategies, keep quiet during games.

✔ Practice sportsmanship. Kids hate it when moms and dads argue with the refs or umps.

Not only do such disputes slow the game down, but it's also embarrassing.

✔ Don't yell out instructions. Especially if your instructions are totally opposite of what the coach has told the kids to do.

✔ After a loss, kids don't like it when you tell them "That's okay — it doesn't matter." Says one kid: "I hate when we get knocked out of the playoffs and my parents say, 'That's okay — you'll get 'em next time!'"

✔ Some parents take the losses much more seriously than their kids do. Then it's up to the kid to cheer up the mom and dad. Kids don't like having to do that.

✔ Parents tell kids "to go out and have fun" playing sports. But if the kids don't take the game seriously, the parents get upset with our easy-going attitude. Mom and Dad, make up your mind!

(Source: *SI For Kids* SportsParents.com, April 1999)

Try to see it from the kid's point of view. Say he's in the fifth grade and is playing basketball. Most likely, the child has been playing hoops for a few years, enjoys the game, and most likely can't wait for the next game on the schedule. The kid is usually smart enough to realize that he's just in fifth grade — which means that he'll have a lot more basketball games to play next year, and the year after that, and the year after that, and so on.

So from the kid's vantage point, he's just on a long continuum of playing games. He's not worried about doing well enough to make it to the NBA, or college, or even the high school varsity. He's just looking ahead to the next game. This perception of the future plays heavily into his active enthusiasm for playing and enjoying the game. And it's a perception that too few parents understand.

Steve Young, the All-Pro quarterback of the San Francisco 49ers, has often been quoted about when he was growing up playing youth sports in Greenwich, Connecticut. Young often recalls that he was just looking forward to his next game: He didn't worry about making the high school football team until he was in high school, and he didn't worry about making his college team until he went to college. In fact, Young didn't even think of seriously playing in the National Football League until he was a junior in college. Steve says that all during those years he was just concentrating on having fun playing ball.

This story is typical of many top athletes today. No mother or father actively pushed the youngster to become the best athlete the world has ever seen. That kind of approach rarely works. Instead, especially in the early years (ages 4 through 10), it's much more important that you let your child simply enjoy the game, learn the rules, master the fundamentals, and most importantly, develop a love for it.

If your child doesn't develop a love for a sport early in his career, he's not going to be motivated to go out and practice his skills on his own when he's a teenager.

Chapter 2

Determining the Right Age to Begin Sports

*D*oes the following sound familiar?

> ✔ "Hey, you ought to see my 3-year-old swing a baseball bat! He's a natural! But then again, I've been working with him since he was 6 months old. . . ."
>
> ✔ "My little girl just fell in love with figure skating and wants to compete in the sport. But she's already 5 years old . . . isn't she too old to start training now?"
>
> ✔ "Our 7-year-old doesn't seem to have much interest in sports. Should we just give up on him in terms of athletics?"

Yikes! These are, of course, common concerns of parents, but in effect they're suggesting that their kids are "washed up" or "has-beens" if they aren't playing sports and starring in them by the time they're 8 or 9. It's a pretty sad commentary if we come to the conclusion that our youngsters just aren't going to cut it in athletics if they haven't been consumed by sports in their earliest years. Many parents seem to believe that if a youngster doesn't get on the "fast track" in sports at an early age, then the child's chance to develop into a top high school, collegiate, or professional athlete will simply vanish into thin air.

And of course, lots of top athletes today were introduced to their sport at a very early age. Tiger Woods is often pointed to as an example of a youngster who was introduced to the game of golf at the age of 3. Wayne Gretzky first started on ice skates when he, too, was a similar age.

But as a parent, bear in mind the following two points as you give your newborn a hockey puck as a teething ring or teach him how to chip a shot before he can walk:

✔ You hear only about those athletes who ultimately made the grade as top professionals. What you *don't* hear about are those youngsters who started out very young, but who never made it, becoming victims of burnout, boredom, a lack of talent, or even more sadly, a pushy parent.

Take the example of Beverly Klass, who made her LPGA debut when she was all of 9 years old. As a fourth-grader from Encino, CA, Beverly drove a golf ball 223 yards and made her pro debut at the Dallas Civitan Open. By all accounts, Beverly was a child prodigy in golf shoes — and she loved it. Problem was, her dad, Jack Klass, quickly assumed that if his daughter went on to even greater success, more fame and fortune would follow. So, to accomplish that goal, the father pushed, prodded, and pulled Beverly to the point where golf was no longer fun, but just a job — and a difficult job at that. By the time Beverly was 13, despite her golfing talents, she had had enough of the game and her dad. She flat out quit. (Source: *The New York Times,* April 8, 1997)

✔ I've never heard any scientific evidence suggest that if a child starts playing one sport at age 5 or younger, he or she has a better chance of becoming a sports star. On the other hand, I can point to lots of studies that strongly conclude that a youngster who is pushed heavily into playing just one sport while growing up has a good chance of becoming a victim of athletic burnout and may quit playing the sport by the time he or she reaches the age of 13.

Furthermore, dozens of top professional players played all different sports as children before deciding on just one when they were in their teens. And other professional athletes switched sports entirely from the one they started in and still became top athletes.

✔ Tom Glavine, a pitcher for the Atlanta Braves, was drafted out of high school as a hockey player.

✔ Curtis Pride, a long-time major league outfielder, played college basketball at William & Mary.

✔ Jackie Joyner-Kersee was outstanding in both basketball and in track and field when she was in high school and college.

✔ Grant Hill, the NBA All-Star, was a top soccer player when growing up.

✔ Hakeem Olajuwon, another NBA All-Star, was a top flight soccer goalie. He didn't even start playing basketball until he was in his late teens.

✔ World track champion Marion Jones gave up running for four years to concentrate on basketball in college.

✔ Cynthia Cooper, a two-time WNBA MVP, didn't pick up a basketball until she was 16.

When and how does your child start playing sports? Good question. Look at sports over the long-term in the chronology of your child's development. The early years have certain key developmental characteristics. As your child gets older, these developmental abilities shift. By the time the child reaches junior high school, his priorities about sports have shifted many times. As you read any chapter of this book, keep in mind how old your child is. Understanding the focus of his age group goes a long way in helping you cope with the highs and lows in sports.

The Early Years: Ages 1 to 3

The first few years of a child's life bring rapid changes in coordination skills and neuromuscular development. If you bear in mind that an average baby doesn't even learn to take a few steps until the ninth or tenth month of the first year, it's really extraordinary to think that, just a few months after that, he can run freely, throw objects, and start to develop a sense of his body's athleticism.

By the time most children are 3 or 4 (keeping in mind that all kids develop their skills at their own pace!), they are discovering that the concept of "play" is a wonderfully self-satisfying activity. Toddlers often repeat an action many times if they can elicit a certain response from a toy or gadget. For example, a 4-year-old may find great fun in constantly cranking a jack-in-the-box just to see the clown pop up, over and over again. No matter how many times the child cranks the toy, the child's face always shows great joy. This repetitive action and response reflects the child's appreciation of mastering a skill.

Don't overlook these important events in a child's life because these magical moments are the first inklings of the child's mastery of her environment and how her physical actions (her neuromuscular skills) are causing a pleasurable effect. At first, her focus may be playing with a jack-in-the-box. Within a few months, her attention may turn to rolling a ball on the ground to you. Bit by bit, more skills are developing, until around the age of 4 or 5, the random play activities advance to the first beginnings of group games and sports.

The Learning Phase: Ages 4 to 8

In some communities, kids as young as 4 or 5 are allowed to register and play on local recreational teams. At this young age, the children rarely have the cognitive ability to understand the most fundamental strategy or, for that matter, the rules of the sport. Just watch a bunch of 5-year-olds play in a soccer game and you quickly observe that very few have any understanding of position, passing strategy, or any special skill level beyond occasionally kicking a ball and running after it.

By the time a child is 6, 7, or 8, he is still going through a steep learning process, both in terms of mastering athletic skills and becoming more accustomed to the parameters of the sport. Although coaches may try to explain several times in many ways to a 6-year-old where to play on a baseball diamond, or how to dribble a basketball, only a rare child quickly masters such physical and mental skills.

The majority of kids at this age level are just happy to be wearing a shiny new uniform, to be a member of a team with their friends, and to be running around and having a good time. And you know what? That enthusiasm is really what you want your child to be learning at this stage because unless your youngster develops a true passion for his sport, he's not going to keep pursuing it as he gets older. In short, if it's fun, then the child will keep on playing — ideally, right through middle school and into high school and maybe beyond.

The two keys: patience and praise

These first few years play a vital role in allowing your child to develop a love and passion for physical activity, for learning about competition, for developing a sense of fair play, and of course, for having fun.

As a parent, during these learning years, you can govern your emotions with two major considerations: praise and patience. Without these two key ingredients, your child may not pursue athletics with as much anticipation and fun as he would like.

Patience

When watching your young child develop, you need patience . . . and more patience. Give your child plenty of space and time to learn how to simply enjoy the experience of playing sports, especially during the very early years. That may sound like simple advice, but only the rare mom or dad doesn't give in to the temptation of "Here, Johnny, let me show you how I used to do this when I was a kid. . . ."

Give children the freedom to experiment and try different approaches to their athletic activities. Allow them to express themselves and gain the self-confidence that comes with trying and trying again.

As an adult, have you ever tried an activity or sport that's new to you? What about learning how to ski for the first time? Inline skating? Golf? Whenever you try to master a new skill, you instinctively know that it takes time and patience to develop even the most rudimentary skills to master the sport. It may take weeks, even months, of practice before you can say to somebody, "Yes, I can ski" or "Yes, I can inline skate." And remember that you're viewing all this from the perspective, patience, and judgment of a grown-up!

Now take that adult perspective and put it in the mindset and body of a 4- or 5-year-old. For a little athlete who has never swung a tennis racquet or kicked a soccer ball, these tasks may seem monumentally challenging. The fun, of course, comes both in the repetitive attempts and ultimately, in the successful completion or partial completion (or mastery) of the task.

If you have ever watched a 5-year-old swing a baseball bat and make contact with a pitched ball, you know firsthand how excited and thrilled the child becomes. A sense of self-satisfaction, enthusiasm, and heightened self-esteem instantly results, and a big smile usually highlights such athletic success.

Praise

But patience is only half of the equation. Just as seedlings need both sunshine and water to grow and develop, young athletes need praise and patience. And as they pursue their first few attempts in sports, just having patience is not enough. Praise plays a very big part in keeping them enthusiastic. In effect, the child not only wants to bask in her success of mastering the athletic skill, but she also wants her success acknowledged by a significant person in her life — you.

Praise also is the soothing tonic that helps the youngster who is still struggling with a skill. Just as you may fall, slip, and stumble while learning how to inline skate for the first time, your youngster will most likely struggle a lot in his first attempts. That's where your gentle but sincere praise and encouragement helps to ease his disappointment, wipe away his frustration, and keep her pushing ahead to conquer that athletic skill.

Praise is the motor oil that keeps your child's athletic engine running. Without enough praise, the engine can begin to sputter and stop. So get in the habit early of knowing how to praise your young athlete so that she knows she's on the right track in sports.

> **Question:** It's easy to praise a kid who's a natural in sports — the kind of youngster who picks up everything quickly and easily. But what kind of praise do you give to the child who doesn't handle each sporting activity with instant success?

Answer: You always praise the *effort* — not necessarily the outcome. That is, let the child know that you recognize that he is working hard at riding that two-wheeler, or that she is working hard at learning how to catch a pop-up. That's the key. Let children know that you see them working hard.

You can also help children gauge how much progress they've made in their sport. Remind the child how difficult the skill was for him when he was just starting out, and compare that skill level to what it is today. Let kids reflect for themselves on just how far they've come.

"Mike, I just want you to know that I saw you working out there in the backyard this afternoon on dribbling a soccer ball, and you know what? It's clear to me that you're putting forth quite an effort to master that difficult skill. . . .

"And you know, Mike, you ought to think for a moment about just how far you've come with your dribbling. Remember a few weeks ago? You could hardly dribble the ball at all. Now, thanks to your hard work, you not only dribble with one foot, but it also looks like you're getting the hang of it with either foot. . . ."

Teaching the ultimate lesson in sports

This is also the time that you can introduce your child to the ultimate lesson in youth sports: When it comes to sports, all that matters is that he or she do his or her best.

Winning or losing isn't something that kids can always control. But they can control what kind of effort they put forth. And if they know that they have made a solid effort to perform well, then that is all that anyone can ever ask of them, and more importantly, that's all that they should ever ask of themselves.

A 4- or 5-year-old may not fully comprehend this lesson yet. But make this theme part of your basic sports mantra to your child as she gets older and grows through sports. Yes, she may still shed tears if her team doesn't win the big game, or if she feels that she didn't play well in a certain situation. That happens in sports. But she can develop a sense of what to ask of herself and her abilities as she goes through the sporting ups and downs that all athletes go through.

Teaching kids how to have fun

Parents always want their children to have fun when playing sports. That sounds simple enough.

But to accomplish that goal, you have to give these little ones the space they need to try, fail, experiment, and ultimately, find their way. Let him laugh if he runs up to a soccer ball, takes a big swing with his leg, but falls on his fanny. Or if she hits a ball but then runs around the bases in the wrong direction. Or even if they're chatting with their friends on the bench and not really paying attention to what's going on in the game. Hey, at this tender age, that's all okay! Why? Because your kid is having fun!

As a parent, you may feel a strong urge to focus their attention, to make them concentrate their energies and "take this sport seriously." But if a child who is just learning to enjoy a sport is told to take it seriously, how much fun will that be? A child has plenty of time to start polishing skills and learning the strategies of the game, but when you're only 7 or 8, all you want to do is run around, see your friends, and have fun. And as a parent, it's your job to let your child do just that.

Coping with parental expectations

Even at the earliest ages, a certain portion of the parents in your community may feel that the sooner the "more athletic" kids are placed in a more competitive situation, the more "progress" these children will be able to make. This kind of early-age "athletic pushing" can take several forms, including:

✔ Younger kids are allowed, and even sometimes pushed by their parents, to play against older competition. That is, a 6-year-old may be playing on a team which is composed of 7- and 8-year-olds.

✔ Special coaches or tutors are hired to help those kids who exhibit special skills. These coaches may also run summer camps designed only for the more competitive player.

✔ Travel teams are formed, in which the "more athletic" kids are asked to play on a more competitive team.

Remember that I'm still talking about *children* — ages 4 to 8. But even at these early stages, many parents fall prey to a mythological competitive track that suggests that if you want your child to grow up to become one of the better players, then he or she had better try out for all these travel teams and go to all the special coach's clinics and camps in order not to fall behind the curve when it comes to sports.

You may not recognize where this kind of "keeping-my-kid-up-with-the-Jones kid" mentality starts, but it's certainly easy to understand: What parent doesn't want his child to be considered one of the more gifted athletes in her age group? However, keeping your child ahead of the athletic curve can become an obsession that, ironically, can lead to the child's burning out from the sport and walking away from it as young as 12 or 13.

Although it's okay to have your own dreams for your child, don't let those dreams cross over into your child's world. Remember: This is your child's life. Placing expectations on him to make a travel team at an early age, to take the game seriously all the time, or to focus only on winning as a way of having fun is usually too demanding on your child.

Don't worry about how skilled your child may become when she is this young. Those concerns will take care of themselves as the child matures and starts high school. At this point in her athletic career, all you really want her to do is enjoy the sport because it's simply fun.

"But I don't want to play!"

So what happens when your child tells you on game day that she doesn't want to play — that she would rather stay home and watch television? Or that she doesn't feel well, even though just 15 minutes ago she was doing cartwheels?

These reluctant protests happen more often than you may think. The trick in handling these situations is not to ignore your child's complaints, but rather to sit down with him and try to engage him in a conversation to find out what the real problem may be.

Instead of a head-on, confrontational approach ("Hey, come on, what's wrong with you? How come you don't want to play?"), try a more understanding style. For example: "Gee, Sarah, I'm a little concerned as to why you've decided you don't want to play anymore. I mean, just last week, you couldn't wait to get to the field.")

The typical response is something like, "I don't care . . . I don't want to play anymore." At this point, you want to probe gently but with a real direction: "Well, that's fine, but we'll have to tell the coach and the rest of the kids why you've decided to quit the team . . . what can we say?"

Such an approach starts to teach the essence of team commitment, but more importantly, it provides an opportunity for the little one to finally express his true feelings: "I'm quitting because the coach is mean to me" or "There's a kid on the team who constantly teases me" or "I'm not being given a chance to play the position I want to play."

Regardless of the reason, once you have uncovered it, it's a whole lot easier to help your child cope with the problem. When kids are between ages 4 to 8, their level of sophistication is still fairly limited, and it won't take long to find the reason that they don't want to play; then you can do something about it.

"I don't want to get hurt"

Sometimes a child doesn't want to play because he or she has built up a fear about being physically injured. Perhaps the week before she was accidentally knocked down in a game or practice, and scraped a knee. Or he got hurt in a collision with another kid. Or the child is a bit smaller than the other kids, and she doesn't want to admit it, but she's a little bashful about getting hurt.

Try the same approach as in the "But I don't want to play!" section. Have a mature, one-on-one discussion with your child. Be calm and sympathetic. Once you can get her to talk about her fears, you can start to help alleviate them. You can acknowledge that accidents sometimes happen in sports, but you can also reassure her that it's okay to be a little scared. After a child gets a little older and more sure of herself, she'll be fine.

Real injuries on the field

Parents and coaches often forget that for little athletes, the experience of feeling pain in athletic competition — even if the pain is merely momentary — is a new and scary proposition. A kid trips and falls on a soccer field. A youngster is knocked down in a hockey game. A ball takes a bad hop in softball and clips the kid's arm.

All of these "injuries" are, of course, routine and simply part of the game. But for the young athlete, that moment of pain can bring a whole mix of emotions: pain, fear, embarrassment, and tears. Plus, kids are not certain what they should do, except lie there and hope that somebody comes and takes care of them.

Most times, all the injured child needs is for the coach or the parent to come out on the field, make certain that he's okay, give the little one a few moments to regain his composure (reassure the child that there's nothing wrong with tears), and then ask the child if he wants to come out of the game.

If the child comes to the conclusion that he's all right, then as long as you're certain that he's not injured, it's fine to let him continue. Obviously, if you have *any* concern at all as to the child's health (especially if he bumped or injured his head), then remove the child from the game immediately. Ideally, a doctor or nurse or some other trained medical professional at the game can quickly attend to the child.

More times than not, however, the child will spring back to his feet and claim that he's fine and ready to keep on playing. As long as you're certain (and the parents are certain) that the child is physically okay, then there's no reason not to let him go back and play. Again, common sense is your best bet.

For more serious injuries, call an ambulance immediately. It's helpful if somebody always brings a cell phone to the games, just in case. And if you are coaching, it's always a good idea to find out if any of the parents attending the game are medically trained — just in case.

Imagined injuries on the field

Occasionally, a young athlete may combine a bit of fear along with a touch of hysteria to produce a feigned injury. This situation happens with young athletes because they are still learning how to gauge just how serious an injury may or may not be. It's not uncommon for a youngster to fall to the ground, scream out in agony because of the "injury," but then in a matter of moments, the tears quickly vanish, the smiles return, and she is ready to resume playing.

Reassuring the child that she is physically fine is key at this moment. Let her regain her balance and normal breathing pattern and perhaps drink a bit of water. After you're convinced that she's okay, then it's fine to let her return to the game.

Sometimes the "injury" doesn't happen on the field. A child may tell you on game day, "I don't feel well" or "my back hurts" or "my head hurts." These indiscriminate injuries or illnesses, which are vague at best, often indicate an underlying reason that the child doesn't want to show up at the field.

After you have determined that the child doesn't have a fever, or any reason for a sore back or sore head, then you can probe gently into what's troubling the child.

Be particularly wary if your child tells you about a vague disorder which prevents him from playing — and then 15 minutes later, the child is running around in the house, seemingly without a care in the world. That's always a good tip-off that your youngster is masking some inner reason that he doesn't want to play in the game today.

Boys and girls playing together?

One of the positive developments in recent years is that more girls than ever before are playing sports. Thanks to the impact of Title IX (the law that called for equal opportunities for women at public institiutions), plus the more open attitudes of moms and dads everywhere, girls are finally being recognized as athletes. Even better, each new generation of little boys also recognizes that their female classmates are good athletes as well.

I asked my son John, when he was 9, who the fastest kid was in his grade. "That's easy, Dad — the fastest runner is Michelle." Exposing my outdated perspective, I asked the question again, as though I hadn't heard him properly. Again, he gladly volunteered, "Michelle — we all had races one day in gym class, and she's definitely the fastest kid."

Playing with the boys at their own game

According to the National Federation of State High School Association — which is the governing body of high school sports in this country — in the 1997-98 academic year, 779 girls played varsity football, 1,262 girls played baseball, and 1,907 girls wrestled on boys' team.

And dozens more played on boys' high school ice hockey teams. For example, when Kathy Waldo grew up in Cross Plains, Wisconsin, she loved playing ice hockey. She not only played at Middletown High School with the boys, she ended up being a captain of the team. Kathy, who stands 5-2, 110 pounds, and happens to be afflicted with cystic fibrosis, just finished a four-year ice hockey career at Northeastern University where she was one of the star scorers for the Huskies.

(Source: *USA TODAY,* February 4, 1999; and *Sports Illustrated,* March 8, 1999)

This is good news — that boys today openly acknowledge that girls can be great athletes. Nevertheless, even though in many communities boys and girls start out on the same teams in Little League or basketball or soccer, by the time they're in third grade or older, the teams become segregated by gender.

You won't find a definitive or correct answer for when single-gender teams should exist. And you can find lots of contemporary examples of where girls continue to play on traditionally boys' teams, including football, baseball, ice hockey, and even wrestling at the high school varsity level. According to the latest statistics, hundreds of high school girls are competing with boys in these sports at the varsity level (see the "Playing with the boys at their own game" sidebar for more information).

Flashes of Athletic Brilliance: Ages 9 to 12

By the time young athletes are 9 or 10, they're starting to exhibit the first real flashes of athletic mastery and ability. They're also beginning to show a cognitive understanding not only of the game, its rules, and some of its strategies, but also how those strategies can help them win instead of lose. A sense of competition begins to bubble up inside them as they start to figure out for themselves which opponents are better-than-average players and which ones are not. Kids begin to develop a sense of "fair play" — a fundamental belief that the game should be played fairly and that the rules should be strictly followed in order to ensure a fair outcome. And they fully embrace the ego gratification of being recognized as a youngster who definitely shows some athletic talent and can perform a task well (for example, shooting a foul shot, kicking a soccer ball with either foot, being able to throw strikes over the plate, and so on).

This athletic development continues to build even more during ages 11 and 12. The flashes of athleticism become even more consistent in their appearance, and the youngster begins to get a handle on how to repeat these athletic skills over and over again. A child's personal sense of efficacy with these skills makes him feel good about himself, about the effort he has put into mastering these skills, and any child enjoys any attention or praise from the coach, an adult, or mom and dad.

The beginnings of fair play

As children reach the age of 9 or 10, along with their physical maturation comes a strong sense of fair play and "playing by the rules." Unlike earlier ages, when children either don't know the rules or don't challenge them, at this age (around third or fourth grade) they develop a better understanding of the rules, of right and wrong, and of fair play. In other words, during a course of a game, a 9-year-old athlete may have a tough time coping with a ref's or ump's "bad call." Or she may have great difficulty if one soccer team has 11 players on the field while her team (because of a lack of players) can field only 10. Or if the players on one side think that, somehow, their team's effort has been shortchanged, this may become a major issue that has to be resolved before the competition can be resumed.

I call this the *law and order phase,* and many kids go through it. It's as though they feel they are personally responsible for the outcome of the game, and to ensure a positive outcome, they have to "police" any perceived wrongdoings, especially when it comes to making calls on the field, rule interpretation, or any other potentially controversial situation. In effect, they'll start to challenge the grown-ups who are making the calls.

This phase is just that — a phase — a precursor of adolescence when young teens begin to challenge grown-ups and other aspects of grown-up life. But when they're only 9 or 10, it's important not to simply brush them off, but to take a few moments to explain the reasoning behind each call or move.

Most of the time, children listen and learn what's being explained. They may not like the call or the reasoning, and they may disagree with it, but once they have had their say, they'll return to the game and play on. And by the time children are 11 or 12, they understand how games are played, and that sometimes bad calls or unjust rulings are indeed just part of the game. Problems occur only when a youngster doesn't want to accept these kinds of situations; then true concerns about his or her sportsmanship may pop up.

Who teaches sportsmanship?

In most youth sports leagues, the coaches merely enforce sportsmanship and rarely teach it.

For example, at the end of the game, the two opposing coaches have all the kids line up and shake hands in a perfunctory fashion. Or they show some other act of "sportsmanship." However, because the coach rarely explains the theory behind sportsmanship to the children, the parents need to take on this vital task. And that conversation should take place at home, away from the fields of competition.

When teaching your child about sportsmanship, ask the following kinds of open-ended questions:

✔ How do you feel when your team wins a close game? How do you feel when your team loses a close game? (Get them to articulate their emotions about both the highs and lows of winning and losing.)

✔ How would you feel if, after a tough loss, a kid from the other team poked fun at you and your team?

✔ Have you ever seen an opposing player trash-talk or taunt another player during a game? Do you think that's acceptable?

✔ What about a lopsided game in which one team runs up the score on the other? Do you think that's okay?

✔ What do you think when you see a coach — a grown-up — throw a tantrum during a kids' game? How does that make you feel?

The point of this exercise is to help the child extend the concept of sportsmanship far beyond the athletic world and into the real world; it shows the youngster that there's a right and a wrong way to behave in these kinds of difficult situations.

Ernie Banks, the great baseball Hall of Famer, once observed that "You can't tell if you're a good sport until you lose." That may be a tough lesson for a little one to learn, but it's absolutely true: It's a lot easier to be a "good sport" after you have won a game or a competition. Explain to your child that the basic premise in sports is that if you compete, there's always a chance you may win and a chance you may lose. Don't wait for the child's coach to teach this vital aspect of sportsmanship: As a parent, you need to teach it and enforce it. (See Chapter 11 for more ideas on how to get started.)

During these years, a loss or disappointing performance may be accompanied by tears. Nothing can melt a parent's heart faster than to see your child's eyes well up with tear drops. What do you do? Be kind, sympathetic, and supportive.

There's nothing wrong with your child crying because he feels that he didn't do well. The old macho days of, "Hey, I don't ever want to see my kid cry!" are long gone. (Heck, I always see Hall of Fame athletes cry on television when they are retiring from their sports!) Besides, after you reassure the child, then the tears dry up quickly and she's on to her next challenge.

Enforcing a sense of sportsmanship

If, for some reason, your child doesn't want to accept the basic rules of good sportsmanship and becomes rebellious about it, then, depending on the child's age, you must take some actions as a parent to make certain that these lessons are learned. Follow these steps:

1. **Take a few moments to explain to the child that there are certain fundamental rules of behavior that have to be followed in any sporting competition, and unless these rules are followed, the child won't be allowed to compete.**

2. **If this conversation doesn't have the desired impact on the child, you may have to take a more drastic step, and simply keep him from playing in the next game.**

   This move is not meant to punish the child, but rather to let him know (at an early age) that the issue of sportsmanship is not an issue to be taken lightly. Even though the child will probably perceive such a move as a punishment, the alternative is unacceptable: the child concludes that one can play and still be a "poor sport."

As a parent or coach, you control only one aspect of your child's sport — his or her actual playing time in the game. Taking away some of that time may seem a bit severe, but in the long run, kids will get the point that if they want to play (and believe me, they all want to play), then they'll have to play by the rules of good sportsmanship.

Acquiring a sense of commitment

During these years, a young athlete has to be introduced to the idea of making a commitment to the team. While the term "commitment" may have been bounced around at home when the child was 6 or 7, there really is no need at those tender ages to lean on the concept and enforce it. Pushing a child at those ages during every practice and every game is kind of silly; besides, it gives the child the wrong sense that playing sports is more of an obligation or chore than a chance to have fun.

But by the time they're 9, 10, and older, kids understand what it means to sign up for a team and, in effect, tell the coach (and the rest of the team) that they're going to be a solid member of the team. That means commitment, including getting up early on rainy days and getting to practice on time. It also means scheduling homework and other extracurricular obligations properly so that one doesn't have to miss a game. And, if the child has a conflict in her schedule, then she (and not you) has to call the coach a few days ahead of the conflict to explain why she can't be at the practice or game that weekend. If you make that call, then you're not helping your child develop the necessary self-discipline and commitment.

Like sportsmanship, commitment is an important developmental trait that transcends the athletic field. Living up to one's commitment is all about self-discipline, and it teaches children that if they make promises, then they need self-discipline to carry through on those promises.

TIP

As with sportsmanship, don't wait for the coach to teach about commitment to the team. That's part of your job as a sports parent, and if you have any reason to suspect that your child is taking his commitment to a sports team lightly, then take the time to sit down with him and explain what this promise means.

However, sometimes a child decides halfway through the season that she's not enjoying the experience. Can she quit?

If, for whatever reason, it's clear that your child really isn't happy being on the team, then there are a few steps to follow:

1. **Sit down and have a serious discussion with your youngster as to why she wants to stop playing.**

   She *must* be able to articulate a good reason: simply saying "I don't know" or "I don't like it anymore" is not enough. Gently get her to articulate the real reason that she doesn't want to continue. This approach lets the child know that she can't take her commitment lightly.

2. **Have a conversation with the coach of the team.**

   Explain to him or her what your child's concerns are, and see if there is any way to resolve these problems. By working *with* the coach, in most cases, you can easily remedy the child's reasons for wanting to quit the team.

3. **If it does become clear that, even after all this discussion, the child wants to stop playing, make the reasons known to the coach.**

   Ask your child if he truly understands about commitment, and ask how he expects to handle the next commitment he makes. The process is about developing your child's self-discipline.

Developing discipline

In addition to self-discipline, which pertains to the youngster's desire and dedication to keep performing in sports, your child also needs to develop the discipline to adhere to the rules as put forth by the coach.

Between the ages of 9 and 12, a child encounters a fairly uniform set of rules of discipline from coaches. This may also be the first time that the child is playing for a coach who may not be a neighborhood father or mother, but is actually an independent educator or professional coach.

Both situations can test a pre-adolescent in terms of his dedication and desire to play sports. The best approach as a parent is to always explain to your child ahead of time what to expect — and what is expected of him. Especially as he begins to climb the pyramid of competitive sports, he needs to understand that the coach is — like any teacher in school — somebody worthy of respect and attention.

As a parent, you have to give the coach some time and space to carry out a coaching plan. As a child, the youngster has to adhere to the coach's game plan. If your child doesn't understand this fundamental relationship between coach and player, your athlete may be in for a rough time. After all, the coach is the one who decides who gets the most playing time, and the sooner your child (and you) understands this basic reality of sports, the better off everybody will be.

Young, Independent Athletes: Ages 13 and Older

When the youngster reaches adolescence, many aspects of their athletic pursuits may change — and change dramatically. As a sports parent, always bear in mind that the teenage years are a time of great extremes in a youngster's life — not only in terms of sports, but in terms of physical, intellectual, and emotional growth. As you know from your own adolescent years, this is a time of great transitions in life.

It's also a complicated time because in some middle schools, cuts are first introduced in making a school-based team. Although some athletes may have been already exposed to travel team cuts, in many cases, the middle school athletic experience is the first time a coach who represents the school is given the opportunity and the responsibility of evaluating young athletes.

Some school districts avoid making cuts during the seventh and eighth grades, and instead may offer an intramural program so that all the kids, regardless of ability, can play. Coaches and parents have good arguments on both sides of the question of which policy on cuts works best for the kids.

By the seventh and eighth grades, the youngsters who have both inherent athletic talent as well as a desire to improve their athletic skills continue to develop these abilities during this time. At the other end of the athletic spectrum, some kids, recognizing that perhaps their strengths lie somewhere other than sports, begin a process of self-evaluation as to whether they want to continue competitively in sports, or perhaps find another extracurricular activity to pursue.

This evaluation of athletic interests is part of the process of burgeoning self-awareness. If your child decides that playing competitive sports is not something she's going to shine in, that's fine. Sit down with her, listen to her thoughts, and then ask if she'd like to pursue some other sports or athletic exercises. These may include self-paced athletic activities, such as hiking, dance, biking, and so on. Above all, help your child understand that staying physically fit is not just a convenience — it's an essential part of staying healthy for life.

On the other hand, suppose your child, at age 13, is neither a top athlete nor one of the kids who wants to leave competitive sports, but is somewhere between these two extremes. A substantial number of kids in this middle range enjoy playing sports, want to continue playing sports, but may not strike the casual observer as being an outstanding athletic competitor. Kids in this middle group need plenty of positive feedback to continue in sports because as adolescence works its magic over the next few years, everything can change so dramatically with each young athlete. And if these "average" kids don't keep playing competitively, then they won't enjoy some of the long-range benefits of being a teenage athlete.

As a parent, you know that puberty can change a substantial part of the physical landscape in terms of young athletes. As soon as those hormones kick in, you notice amazing physiological changes with youngsters: Short kids can grow tall, heavy kids can become skinny, slow kids can become fast, skinny kids fill out, and so on.

The truth about travel teams

Around the age of 9 or 10, the option of competing in travel teams may appear on the child's athletic horizon. As I discuss in detail in Chapter 4, travel teams are usually highly competitive teams whose members are chosen based on tryouts. Both the parent and the child have to first sit down and decide whether they want to compete for a travel team. It's important for the parent to do some homework first before allowing the child to put his or her athletic prowess on the line and try out for a travel team.

When former professional basketball player Bob Bigelow was 11 and 12, he described himself as just another kid who liked to play basketball. He certainly wasn't a star; just another skinny kid who was drawn to the game. "Thank goodness they didn't have cuts or travel teams in my town," reflects Bigelow today, who is now in his 40s and a nationally-recognized sports parenting advocate, "because if they did, I wouldn't have made the first cut. I don't know what I would have done without basketball."

But when Bob became a teenager, he started to grow. And because he was getting taller and because he had continued his love for the game, by the time he was in ninth grade, he had progressed to being one of the best players in the school. By the time he was a senior, he was recognized as being one of the best players in the state. And by the time he graduated from the University of Pennsylvania, he had made All-Ivy League status and was a first round draft choice of the National Basketball Association.

Young athletes of 14 and older, now entering high school, have usually decided on their own whether they want to continue to compete in sports at the freshman, junior varsity, or varsity level.

The student-athlete ultimately makes the decision as to whether he or she wants to continue in competitive sports. As a parent, you can certainly offer some guidance to help your child decide, because trying out and committing to a high school team does involve a serious amount of after-school time. Use your experience as an adult to point out to your child what the choice means in terms of self-sacrifice, dedication, and discipline to play for a school team.

Don't have this conversation with your child on the day she tries out for the varsity team, but several weeks, even months, in advance of the decision.

High school sports bring a set of new priorities. For example, unlike the early years where winning should be nowhere near the top priority, at the high school varsity level, winning becomes a greater priority for the coach and the kids on the team. By this time in the student-athlete's career, he or she usually accepts that being victorious in a sporting event is what the team and the coach are shooting for. Nevertheless, the smart coach understands that the fun still resides in playing the game, not just for the top performers, but for all of the players on the team.

"Playing Up" a Gifted Athlete

Sometimes, a child is so gifted that she finds that competing against kids her own age is no longer a challenge. When this happens, her parents often suggest that she *play up* — that is, move up and out of her own age bracket and play against kids who are a little older.

This situation often presents itself with kids between the ages of 8 and 12, and it usually happens because a child's skills are a bit advanced for his age and because he is big for his age. The combination of advanced skills and size makes him too dominant a force in his own age bracket.

Although there's nothing inherently wrong with allowing a child to play in an older bracket, you need to bear in mind a few considerations. Start by asking the child what *he* wants to do. Too many parents instinctively assume that having their children play up a division is such an honor that they (the parents) shouldn't give any thought to it. Like being named to a travel team, too many proud parents assume that having their children play up puts them on the fast track to a collegiate or professional sports career.

But kids who dominate in their own age bracket often aren't as sure as their parents about moving up. Although at first they're excited about being "selected" to play against older kids, their original enthusiasm tends to die down after the practices and games begin.

The truth is, many of these talented kids prefer playing with their same-age friends, not because they can dominate but simply because they enjoy playing and competing with their close friends from school.

These athletes who play up often have other concerns. They may begin to feel great internal pressure to succeed when they are competing against bigger, stronger, and older kids. When these younger "wonderkids" don't dominate at the higher level, they may think that they've failed — or at least, failed their parents. In short, you, as the parent, have to consider the psychological dynamics carefully before you let your 9-year-old play on a team with 11- and 12-year-olds.

Moving a child up — especially a child under the age of 12 — can be somewhat precarious. Try this instead: Have your athlete play within her own age bracket during games, but let her practice occasionally with older kids. In this fashion, she still gets to enjoy social time with her friends, but in terms of athletic development, she can work out with older kids without feeling the pressure of being pushed too hard and too soon.

Take time to consider whether you want to move your talented youngster up to a higher level. Be careful not to let your own emotions rule your decisions. Always take a step back and try to decide what's in your child's best interest.

Chapter 3

Dealing with Your Child's (And Your Own) Disappointments

- -

In This Chapter

▶ Coping with a child in tears

▶ Avoiding the post-game analysis

▶ Offering your kids a praise sandwich

▶ Competing at the top levels of sports

- -

*W*hen your child trots out onto the field or onto the court, you're eager to see him or her perform well. Like any parent, you want your child to succeed and enjoy himself or herself. But what happens when things don't go their way? Many times, parents become understandably perplexed and confused with the whole spectrum of emotional issues that can befall a child athlete, such as

✔ "My 6-year-old seems more interested in picking daisies than kicking the soccer ball when it comes her way."

✔ "My son breaks into tears if he doesn't get a hit in a Little League game."

✔ "The coach cares only about winning, and plays only his favorite kids when the score is close."

✔ "My child is not one of the bigger kids, and he's afraid of getting hurt. What do I do?"

✔ "I don't understand why the league has to cut kids from a team at such an early age. What do I tell my child if she gets cut?"

What do you say to an 8-year-old who has struck out for the third time in a game and is on the verge of tears? Likewise, what's the best way to handle an 11-year-old who has scored her fifth goal in the same soccer game and is beginning to show off a bit too much? This chapter helps you cope with one of the most vexing problems for sports parents — how to react to their children's ups and downs in sports.

Kids take their behavioral cues from their parents and coaches. Given that reality, the question is not so much how kids react to the peaks and valleys of sports, but rather how parents react to their children's ongoing series of achievements and failures.

Monitoring your child's reactions takes time, patience, and a lot of communication. And it's just as important as teaching kids the proper fundamentals or skills of each sport. Smart coaches and sports parents know when and how to make their little athletes feel good about themselves — especially when things aren't going their way on the athletic field. Those same coaches and sports parents know when to bring those talented athletes back down to earth when the youngsters start showing signs of having too big an ego.

When Personal Goals Aren't Met

Every great athlete faces adversity at one point or another in his career. (If there's one universal experience in sports, this may be the most common.) As a parent or coach, you have to take a step back and remind yourself that *all* athletes — even the top professionals — had to struggle with at least one aspect of their sport when they were growing up. Adversity is just part of the experience, and it affects all young athletes. The key is not to try to keep kids from experiencing difficult moments — making an error, giving up a tough goal, making a mental mistake on the field — but rather to help your child understand that these moments occasionally occur, and to learn from these disappointments. Kids can learn how to come back from a tough situation and mentally train themselves to redouble their efforts to try to perform better so that those mistakes and errors don't happen again.

Your 10-year-old basketball player just double-dribbled the ball in the closing seconds of a game. The ball is turned over to the other team, who comes down the court and scores the winning basket. You know your child well. You know that the tears are going to come after the game. What do you do?

1. **First, give your child a hug.**

   Let her cry. There's no reason to chastise her (as in "C'mon, I don't want to see any tears!"). The child's emotions are real. She feels that she let herself and her team down. As a parent, you want to make her feel better.

   You really can't stop the pain. The disappointment is going to hurt. But you can try to minimize the emotional letdown. After the hug, quietly praise your child's effort in the game. Above all, avoid a long lecture! (See the "Avoiding the PGA [post-game analysis]" section for further details.)

2. **Later in the evening, ask your child whether she wants to talk about it.**

   If she does, let *her* do the talking. It's better to allow her to get her feelings out in the open.

3. **After she talks and perhaps cries again, be gently proactive with this parental script:**

"Okay, Sarah, that game is over. Your team lost. You may feel as though you personally lost the game for your team, but really, that's a selfish attitude. Didn't the other players on the team lose the ball on other turnovers? Didn't they miss shots? Didn't they miss rebounds? Didn't they have other opportunities to score baskets?

"So it's over. And if you're going to play sports, you must realize that winning and losing are basic parts of the game. If you play, there's never a guarantee that you're going to win or lose — that's why they play the games. And many times, you can't control that outcome.

"But there are certain aspects of your game that you *can* control. And that's how much effort you put into your practice. Because if you want to succeed in any sport, or any path you choose in life, you have to make up your mind that you have to practice and work at it. If you don't, you can still enjoy playing the game, but you won't necessarily be as successful as you would like. But if you can somehow transform the anger and frustration you feel now into a positive practice session, you'll be that much more prepared for the next game when you have to handle the ball."

Avoiding the PGA (post-game analysis)

One surefire way to ruin your child's enthusiasm for a sport is the PGA — the post-game analysis.

What's the last thing many parents tell their kids when they go off to play sports? "Go have fun!" That's what parents exhort their kids to do.

But then, within minutes of the game or match or competition coming to a close, the little athlete is bundled back into the family station wagon and the post-game analysis begins, with questions like the following:

- ✔ "Sally, what happened on that shot you missed?"
- ✔ "Michael, you didn't seem to be hustling today . . . was there a problem?"
- ✔ "Samantha, it didn't look like you really wanted to win today . . . ."

This is the kind of post-game grilling that most professional athletes don't tolerate in a press conference, so why do you expect your child to enjoy it? How come they have to be criticized? After all, wasn't the last thing you told him or her to do was to go out and have fun? And now, a couple hours later, you're going to go through a detailed performance evaluation?

"I go through this process right after the game," say some parents, "because the game is still fresh in my child's mind, and it's easier for him to remember it."

Baloney. Most parents want to go through the PGA simply because the game is still fresh in *their* minds, and they want to get their own frustrations off their chests.

The bottom line is this: If you keep going through PGAs with your child after each competition, pretty soon you'll discover that your child becomes quiet in these sessions; only answers in short, perfunctory tones; or just loses interest in talking with you about the game. That ruins it for everybody.

I suggest that you give your kid some time to relax and unwind. You can chat about the competition and the experience of it all, but there's no reason to go into detail about it. Wait until the evening, perhaps after dinner when there's a quiet time. Then, ask your child what *she* enjoyed the most about the event that day, how she felt she performed, and what she remembers the most. In other words, the key here is not *you* giving a detailed analysis or lecture, but rather, letting *your child* draw you into the conversation. Ask her open-ended questions so that she's given the opportunity to talk as much as she wants.

This approach works wonders. If you give your child the freedom to express herself about the experience, you usually find that she truly enjoys sharing her thoughts with you. Instead of being seen as a tough-minded coach and critic by your child, you're now viewed as a true friend and avid supporter. And that's the relationship you definitely want with your young athlete.

Offering a praise sandwich

So what do you say when you feel it's necessary to offer some "constructive criticism" to your athlete?

What do you say to the child who has become a bit of a "ball hog" in basketball and won't pass the ball to teammates, or the kid who doesn't play in position properly during the game, or the youngster who keeps making up excuses for a poor performance in gymnastics meets?

Feed your child a praise sandwich. A verbal sandwich that consists of two parts of praise surrounding a delicate slice of criticism. Here's an example:

> ✔ **A slice of praise:** "John, there's no question that you've become quite a shooter on the basketball court. When you get an open shot, there's a real good chance that you're going to score . . . ."
>
> This opening bit of praise always gets the child's attention because all kids like being praised and complimented for their skills. The child appreciates that you, as a grown-up, openly acknowledge that he's a good player. That makes the youngster feel good about himself — and about you as well. After you have his attention, give him . . .

✔ **A slice of constructive criticism:** "And you know, Johnny, if you can become as good at passing the ball as well as shooting it, why, there would be no stopping you at all. You'd be a true scoring machine!"

Note that even the criticism is still covered with praise. You want the youngster to really absorb what you have just said. Like taking a bit of sugar with some bad-tasting medicine, you're merely trying to sweeten the taste a bit.

✔ **The final bit of praise:** "Because if you master both the scoring and the passing aspects of basketball, you'd be on your way to having some terrific games. You'd be something really special."

And that's the praise sandwich.

What happens to the youngster who takes a bite?

✔ He realizes that you obviously think he's a good player — that's why you praised him.

✔ He has heard you about becoming a better passer. Instead of rejecting that advice out of hand, he's thinking, "Hmm . . . maybe that's a good point. Maybe I ought to work on my passing more. Because then I would really be a star."

✔ Praising him again provides the inspiration and motivation for him to go out and work on those new passing skills. Which, of course, is what you wanted him to do in the first place.

What's the alternative approach? Sadly, too many times a coach or a parent simply tells the young athlete in a blunt manner: "Hey, stop being such a ball hog — pass the ball to some of your teammates, will ya?" This kind of approach not only demotivates the kid, but it also ruins any rapport between the player and the coach. Ask yourself: What approach would work better for your youngster? Give the praise sandwich a couple of tries and see how it works for you.

Working off the disappointment

Many parents observe that when a child loses a game or feels that he has played poorly, he will go out on his own and practice the sport until he feels that he has purged his body of the disappointment. I have seen kids who, after making a fielding error in a baseball game, take a ball when they get home and throw it against a garage in order to improve their fielding. Or kids may work on their basketball shooting if they miss a lot of shots in a game.

What about incentives?

One father observes, "My 12-year-old son is terrifically talented as an athlete, but he doesn't seem to want to work out or practice that much. He just wants to play in the games. Is there any way I can give him an incentive or motivate him to do more?"

Some parents give their kids constant pep talks. Others push their kids by reminding them how "competitive" the sports world is and that they'd "better be ready" for the next game. Other parents try to motivate their kids by offering financial incentives: "Hit a home run and I'll give you $20!"

The problem is that no matter what you say or promise to do for a young athlete, you can't have much of an effect until she makes up her mind to go out and practice on her own. There are no magic words or special formulas to follow.

In the same way that you can't push children or prod them to be smarter, to be neater, or to read more books, you can't push them to practice their athletic skills. Threatening them, of course, doesn't work. Only when they're ready will they find the inner motivation and drive to go out and work hard.

For most athletes, this process doesn't really set in on a serious level until they reach a certain level of adversity. When a 13-year-old suddenly finds himself on the bench — or worse, cut from the junior high team — he may realize that, if he wants to compete at higher levels, he has to start putting in the long hours that will convert his raw athletic ability into true athletic talent. But again, that's a decision that only the student can make for himself.

As a parent, you should encourage such behavior. Such a practice session accomplishes two vital and immediate goals for children:

- ✔ It allows them to work off their frustration.
- ✔ By practicing those skills that "betrayed" them in their game, they begin to feel that they have reclaimed those skills.

For a young athlete, these are important sessions, not only in terms of getting rid of any residual disappointment, but also in terms of reasserting his mastery of his skills. Nobody knows why some kids turn that frustration into a personal challenge, but if you ever see your child doing just that, relax and rejoice — you have a very special kid.

When Your Child Behaves Badly

The flip side of kids who experience disappointment are the youngsters who dominate their peer groups at an early age. These are the children who quickly score goals (and lots of them) in soccer matches or hockey games, who can't be stopped on the basketball court, or who run over the competition when playing football.

Kids as young as 9 or 10 who begin to realize that they are the stars sometimes develop a warped sense of sportsmanship. You may spot a 10-year-old taunting the less-talented opposition during the course of a lopsided game or saying less-than-complimentary things to the kids on the other team. Or perhaps he won't pass the ball to one of his teammates, preferring to take the majority of the shots himself.

Although seeing one's son or daughter be so athletically gifted fills a parent with great pride, it doesn't make anyone feel good if the child isn't well-trained in sportsmanlike behavior. It's important to recognize that kids aren't born as bad sports — they usually learn these destructive patterns of behavior from watching top professionals on television do unsportsmanlike things.

If you happen to spot your child acting in an unsportsmanlike manner, you (and the coach) have to take immediate action. The best approach is to merely take the athlete out of the game immediately, and explain to her why she was removed from the game. Keep her on the sidelines until she begins to understand that you aren't kidding about this — even if it means sitting out for an extended period of time. (See Chapters 2 and 11 for more ideas on teaching sportsmanship.)

What do you do if the coach doesn't do anything to discipline your child? Take a moment after the game to chat with the coach. Calmly explain to him or her how upset you were with your child's behavior during the game, and how much you would like the coach to remove your child from the game if such actions happen again. Tell the coach that you'll be speaking directly with your child about her inappropriate actions, and that you hope the coach understands your point of view. In other words, take the matter out of the coach's hands. Don't tolerate inappropriate behavior and don't wait for the coach to take immediate action. As a parent, keep in mind that the lesson of sportsmanship starts at home.

Bad sports(wo)manship

Don't think for a moment that rough and crude behavior is strictly the domain of kids.

One woman became so enraged at a call that a referee made in a 12-and-under soccer game that she confronted the ref — a 15-year-old boy — who demanded that she leave the field immediately. She didn't, and then punched the teenage ref in the mouth, splitting his lip.

Her punishment? Banned from attending youth soccer games, sentenced to six months' probation, and given a 15-day suspended jail term. She was also told to pay a $250 fine, perform 50 hours of community service, and — oh yes — write a letter of apology to the youngster.

(Source: *USA Today,* Nov. 19, 1998)

If the child goes back into the game and continues to trash talk or taunt opponents or exhibit other unsportsmanlike acts, remove her again. This time, you can be a lot more forceful in your approach.

Why is this important at this early age? Because if your child doesn't learn the right way to behave in sports when he's a kid, he's rarely going to learn it as he gets older.

When the Future Doesn't Appear to Hold Promise

"It's not where you start, but where you finish that counts" may be considered a sports cliché, but like most clichés, it carries a certain amount of truth. Naturally, it's hard to predict which of today's youngsters may become tomorrow's athletic stars. Becoming a top performer involves just the right combination of innate athletic talent, a competitive attitude, and loads of hard work and practice. If your child is missing any of the following components, it's difficult to predict that she may succeed at her chosen sport in the years to come:

- Superior innate athletic ability
- An extreme desire to succeed
- A personal major commitment to practice and hard work

You can find lots of examples of current top athletes who didn't necessarily exhibit All-Star status as kids but who, deep down, had all three of these components in their makeup. In some, it just took a little time for these elements to reveal themselves and blossom. Remember, everybody grows, develops, and matures at different rates! The teenage years — the prime years for growth in an athlete — go from 13 through 19 — and it doesn't matter whether you grow at age 13 or at age 19. The body goes through amazing changes during these years.

- There's the story of little Mark who, as a Little League baseball player, had difficulty seeing the ball when fielding and hitting because his eyesight was so poor. In fact, Mark had 20/500 vision. But after he had it corrected, he developed into a good high school and college player. Today, the world knows him as Mark McGwire.

- No one saw Mike Gartner, one of the all-time leading NHL goal scorers, as a star when he was growing up in Canada. He was a fast skater, but he wasn't particularly big. But he stayed with the sport because he loved it, and eventually the NHL scouts gave him a chance.

✔ When Billy Wagner was in high school in a small town in Virginia, he stood only 5'3" and weighed only 135 pounds — as a senior! But by the time he entered college a year later, he grew seven inches and another 40 pounds. Now the ace lefthander for the Houston Astros, Wagner is one of the hardest throwing pitchers in the majors today.

✔ Because of a childhood illness, Wilma Rudolph had to wear stiff and uncomfortable leg braces until she was 11 year old. But within a few years of the braces being removed, she won gold medals in the Olympics as the fastest woman runner in the world.

✔ When New York Mets' all-time save leader, John Franco, was in high school, he was so small that his high school coach told him that there was no way he could ever play on the varsity. But that didn't deter Franco, who not only went on to star in high school, but also at St. John's University.

✔ When Cynthia Cooper, two-time MVP of the WNBA, was growing up in the impoverished Watts area of Los Angeles, she found that she had to teach herself basketball when she was 16 years old. There were no leagues or clinics for her to play in. Yet within a matter of a few years, she had made herself into one of the top players in the Los Angeles area.

All of these athletes — and hundreds more just like them — didn't necessarily start off well, but by the time they finished, they were true All-Stars. What drove them (in addition to their talent) was their desire to compete and succeed, and to willingly go through endless hours of practice. Of course, most top athletes can tell you that they truly enjoyed working hard in practice because it was both fun and aimed towards achieving a goal.

"Do your best!"

"Just do your best." This universal bit of parental advice continues to be a constant theme, and as a Mom or Dad of a young athlete — regardless of your child's overall sports ability — this is what you want him to be comfortable with. It makes no difference whether he's destined to become the next NBA superstar or just another kid who likes to swim, hike, and snowboard; all you want him to do is to find a level in sports at which he's comfortable. Because unless children look upon their sporting activity as being fun, joyful, and a challenge they can handle, they're going to eventually turn away from that event.

Wherever your child feels comfortable, the bottom line is still "just do your best." And regardless of your child's athletic ability, he still wants to know you actively support him, root for him, and are proud of his accomplishments. That's what kids want to hear from their parents.

When the Athlete Wants to Quit

As a child finds her own level in sports, there may be times when she comes to you and announces that she's no longer going to play a particular sport:

- ✔ A 7-year-old decides halfway through the soccer season that she doesn't like running up and down the soccer field and wants to quit.

- ✔ A 10-year-old who has played baseball since he was 6 tells you one spring that he wants to play lacrosse instead of baseball.

- ✔ A 13-year-old swimmer has tired of all the long, lonely practice sessions in the pool and wants to give up the sport so that he can focus on trying out for the school play.

As a parent, what do you say and do when a child makes this kind of pronouncement? Here are some steps to follow:

1. **Take your child's decision seriously.**

   Remember, this is his decision, not yours, and as much as it may break your heart that your child has decided on a different course of action, you have to respect him for taking action.

2. **Ask your child to try to articulate the reasons she's not enjoying the sport as much as before.**

   Tell her that there are other issues here besides "I just don't like it anymore" or "I'm not having fun." Particularly with older kids, remind them of having made a commitment to the rest of the team and to the coach.

3. **Take a moment to review the child's involvement in his sport.**

   Talk about the wonderful times he has had, his achievements, the camaraderie, and so forth. Remind him that he's walking away from those times (at least for the time being). Of course, he can always return to that sport next year or the year after, but it's important that you discuss his decision to leave that activity behind.

4. **After the decision has been made, make certain you tell her that you support her at whatever she wants to try next, but that you do want her to try something else to help fill in the hours.**

   Be wary of the child who says that she wants to quit playing a sport just so "I can hang out with my friends" (not a particularly productive activity).

And how many end up quitting?

Recent studies show that more than 73 percent of all kids who play organized youth sports end up quitting by the time they reach the ripe old age of 13. (Source: *Time,* July 12, 1999)

Also be wary if a child tells you that he wants to quit playing a sport because "I need more time with my homework." Again, although this seems like a noble reason, numerous studies show that athletes develop better study habits and time management skills than their non-athletic peers because of having to balance after-school practices with their homework time. So although it's okay for a child to stop pursuing a sport after school, make certain that he's putting all that energy into another productive outlet.

Chapter 4

Evaluating the Pros and Cons of Travel Teams

• •

In This Chapter

▶ Defining travel teams

▶ Dealing with potential burnout

▶ Knowing which vital questions to ask a travel team coach

• •

*U*nlike local school and recreational teams, travel teams are, in effect, All-Star teams. They usually are age-specific (that is, geared to a particular age bracket) and segregated by gender (although in some rare instances, you find the occasional girl playing on a boys' soccer, hockey, or baseball team). In most communities, kids start playing on travel teams at around the age of 8 or 9; in some cases, there are travel squads for kids as young as 6 or 7.

Travel teams in youth sports are a relatively new phenomenon, starting perhaps no more than 15 years ago. Nobody is quite certain where or how they originated, but one characteristic about travel teams is fairly clear: In most communities, a great deal of prestige and pride is attached to being selected for one of these teams. After all, what child wouldn't take special pride in being named to a travel team? The youngster usually gets a new uniform and maybe even a new warm-up jacket from the team, and of course there's the prestige of being one of the "golden children." The tradeoff is that with a desire for prestige and pride comes increased pressure for a child to be one of the chosen. And parents are invariably eager to see their children succeed, not fail, when trying out for a travel team.

Depending on where you live, *travel teams* may also be known as *select, premier, elite, A teams,* and so on. But no matter what they're called in your community, their purpose is fairly clear: These are teams for which children usually have to compete in carefully scrutinized tryouts in order to be selected. Invariably, cuts are involved, and those children who are deemed "not good enough" to make a travel team are informed that they didn't make the cut.

Of course, the intent of a travel team is to give those "selected" children an opportunity to play against other "selected" teams from neighboring towns or communities — hence, the term "travel." Sometimes, the travel can involve as much as several hours each way to play another team; it can even involve a tournament that occurs over an entire three-day weekend. Because a travel team does involve substantially more commitment, both in terms of time and money, than a local recreational team does, ask many questions before you commit your son or daughter to this kind of team — this chapter helps you select the right questions to ask.

Are Travel Teams Really Necessary?

This is the first question that you should be asking — even before you ask yourself whether your child should be trying out for, or playing on, a travel team. In my professional knowledge, no studies indicate or prove that a child's participation on a travel team guarantees his long-range success in that sport.

This is especially true for children under the age of 13 — kids who haven't gone through adolescence yet. Kids go through two major developmental phases in youth sports — before age 13, and after:

- ✔ The first phase is in the early years, ages 4 through 12, when children are first introduced to playing sports and begin to master the neuromuscular skills and techniques needed to play them.

- ✔ The second phase occurs with the onset of adolescence, usually around age 13. During the adolescent years, as youngsters go through a number of physical and emotional changes, their passion for athletics can change dramatically — in either direction. Some kids focus completely on their sports, while others will find that their interest in competitive athletics begins to dwindle.

The parents of young sports enthusiasts can't underestimate the impact of the teen years. During these "magical" years, all sorts of physical and psychological changes can occur: Short kids sprout up seemingly overnight, chubby kids become lean, tall kids stop growing, slow kids become faster, insecure kids gain confidence, and so on. The sports pages of today's newspapers and magazines are filled with the inspirational stories of famed top athletes who really didn't hit their stride in their respective sports until they were well into their teens.

Every school kid knows the legend of Michael Jordan, who, as a sophomore in high school, not only wasn't the star of the varsity, but didn't even make the team! Yet just five years later, Jordan was considered the premier basketball player in the country. How did that happen? Consider that when Jordan was a sophomore, he stood 5'10" tall, and his best sport was baseball. Only by his junior or senior year in high school did he start to grow to his adult height of 6'6".

Too many parents either overlook or forget that kids grow at different rates and at different times. Never underestimate the power of adolescent growth! A lot of things can happen to a kid from the time she is 12 to her 20th birthday.

So here's the bottom line on having your child try out for a travel team. As a parent, understand fully that making a travel team (especially at an age under 12) is never a predictor of continued athletic success as the child reaches their teens in high school. Furthermore, there's always the risk that your child won't end up making the travel team, and that's always a worry for any parent or child. On the plus side, it is true that for the athletically-gifted youngster, playing on a travel team can allow him or her to play against stronger competition for their age bracket. That may allow the child to develop physical skills at a faster pace and to develop more self-confidence in his or her abilities.

Whatever you choose, be certain to weigh the options carefully. And whatever you select for your child, remember that your kids will only derive satisfaction and fun from sports if they are actually playing in games. Recreational teams always guarantee that — travel teams don't always make that promise.

Dealing with Disappointment at Tryouts

As a caring parent, you have to be well prepared when your child comes home from school and tells you that she wants to try out for the travel team. Sit down with her and explain what a travel team involves. Explain the time, the commitment, and the travel, and most importantly, let her know that she has no guarantee of making the team.

For most children, this will be one of the first times in their young lives that they will be auditioning for a team — and they may not be prepared for a bad outcome. It's incumbent upon you — not the coaches who run the tryout — to prepare your child for both good and bad news. No matter which way the tryout goes, try to minimize the outcome. Emphasize to your child that this is just one experience and that as long as she does her best, that's all she can ask of herself. Either way, she's still a terrific little athlete, and you love her.

Travel tryouts differ from sport to sport. Some are held over the course of several hours on a particular Saturday. Sometimes, it's just a scrimmage between the players. Other times, the kids are put through drills and skills. Usually, a team of coaches evaluates to see which kids are going to be chosen. (You usually pay a small fee to have your child try out for the travel team.) But no matter what format the tryouts take, as nervous as the kids are, the parents are even more frantic. This, of course, is understandable, but not very productive. If you can't handle the pressure of watching your child perform, go for a walk or take a drive. Whatever you do, don't let your child see how nervous you are. That will only serve to make her more nervous!

As you can imagine, telling a child under the age of 12 that he didn't make the travel team — in effect, that he didn't make the cut — can be psychologically devastating for the youngster. Tears of disappointment are common. In most cases, this setback is the first time in the youngster's life that he has seen his dreams dashed. Watching your child get cut from the team also places you in a most tenuous situation; specifically, how do you explain to your 8-year-old that she isn't good enough to make the team?

Strong emotions can flow at a time like this, and confrontations between angry parent and coach happen all too often. Charges of "favoritism," "politics," or worse may be leveled by the parent, who may feel that the child has been cheated. And yes, sadly, sometimes these kinds of influences are very much in effect when such teams are selected, and you can do little, as a parent, to intervene. You can seek out the head coach or the director, but usually in this pressurized kind of situation, you rarely obtain satisfactory answers (for example: Was my child too slow? Too small? Why wasn't he good enough?).

Before the tryouts, plan ahead how you want to handle the situation if your child doesn't make the cut. What can you say to make him feel better? Bear in mind that I honestly don't think there's a good way to explain to an 8-year-old why he didn't make a team. That's a conversation I would really like to avoid with my own children.

But such situations do occur. If you find yourself in this predicament, try to remind your disappointed child that this is not the end of the world. And if you have an anecdote from your own past when you were deeply disappointed, this is a good time to share it with your child. But whatever you do, don't minimize the pain that your child is going through.

> Parent: "Sam, I know how disappointed you must be in not making that team."
>
> Child: "I don't understand! I thought I played so well."
>
> Parent: "And you did play well, but you know, they could only take so many kids, and like yourself, a lot of them were very talented. Did I ever tell you about the time I got cut from a team that I tried out for?"

A little personal inspirational story here of how you were disappointed and then came back the following year would be of great solace to your child here. Kids like to be reassured that it's okay to fail, as long as they have another chance to rebound down the road.

Knowing What to Ask a Travel Team Coach

If your young athlete makes the cut and is named to a travel team, you, as a parent, need to step up and start asking questions about what being on this team is going to involve. *Before* you say yes to letting little John or Julie join a travel team, ask the head coach the following specific questions:

- ✔ "What's your philosophy on playing time for all the kids on the team?"

- ✔ "Do you tend to be loud with the children?" (meaning, is the coach a yeller and screamer?)

- ✔ "Do you allow unsportsmanlike behavior, like trash talking or taunting, from the kids?"

- ✔ "How do you discipline the children?"

- ✔ "Is there any punishment if my child misses a practice or game due to a schedule conflict?"

- ✔ "What kind of experience do you have coaching kids of this age?"

- ✔ "Does the team have an assistant coach as well?"

- ✔ "Can I get your telephone number? What's a good time to call you?"

- ✔ "Do you have a roster of kids whom you coached last year?"

Too many parents are intimidated or think that asking a coach these kinds of questions is wrong. Don't make that mistake! Clearing up any confusions or misunderstandings now can go a long way in making certain that your child (and you) fully enjoy the season. Travel teams inherently involve a great deal more commitment in terms of time, distance, and finances than local recreational teams do. So ask the questions *now*.

Keeping It Fun — Even at a Competitive Level

The last bit of advice that most moms and dads give to their children as they jump out of the family station wagon to go play in a game is, "Have fun!" That's sound advice — but it's the rare parent who really allows the child to go out on the playing field and just "have fun."

Instead, after the game begins, the kids can't help but notice that the parents are taking this affair quite seriously. You have probably observed parents yelling and screaming on the sidelines at any youth league game. It doesn't take long for a child of any age to realize that even though Mom and Dad urged them to have fun, the game is obviously a lot more than "just a game." And with travel teams, parents and coaches seem to raise the stakes even higher.

If your son or daughter is on a travel team, there's a good chance that he or she will be exposed to a higher level of expectation by the coach, the other parents, and even the other players. Not all children cope well with this kind of travel team mentality, especially if they're younger than 12. If you have concerns about your child, think twice about letting her participate on a travel team.

Keep in mind, too, that there are big differences between the amount of playing time the average child gets on a recreational league or school team and the amount of time he'll get on a travel team. Travel teams usually crop up in communities in which local recreational leagues already exist. In recreational leagues, any child who registers is able to play on a team, regardless of his ability. In most cases, the league stipulates that every child (again, regardless of ability) must play in at least half the game. It's usually up to the individual coach to figure out a way to make sure that each child plays in the game. In effect, if you pay the registration fee, your child plays.

In contrast, the coach of the travel team is *not* bound by the customary league mandate that everybody plays. Some of the more zealous travel team coaches place a top priority on winning each and every game. These misplaced priorities — lack of equal playing time for all kids and an overwhelming desire to win — can often lead to major crises on travel teams, especially with kids who are younger than 12.

This is why it's so vital that, as a parent of a travel team player, you do your homework before the season and ask questions of the travel team coach. You'll have more difficulty approaching the coach during the season about why your son or daughter is not getting enough playing time or is playing in a different position. Better to know what to expect before the games begin rather than try and fix things after the season is under way.

Looking at Travel Teams and Burnout

Burnout is a term that's applied to young (and often very talented) athletes who decide that they're no longer enjoying playing a particular sport as much as they once did, and simply decide to stop playing it. In the majority of cases, this psychological phenomenon often occurs around the ages of 12 to 15. And it happens more often than parents may expect.

Burnout can occur for several reasons. Perhaps the child is playing in so many games that they're no longer fun; to him, playing the sport has become a chore. Or maybe the child is physically and emotionally exhausted from constantly having to compete and is just tired of having to please Mom, Dad, or the coach on the sidelines. Sometimes, young athletes develop other interests in life and find that a particular sport is no longer their top priority.

Whatever the underlying reason, one observation is clear: The child's original passion for the sport has dwindled to the point where he just doesn't want to go out and play anymore. That's the essence of burnout, and it's a difficult situation for parents and coaches to grapple with.

There seems to be a direct correlation between the recent sprouting of travel teams and kids who suffer from burnout. After all, if your 10-year-old child is on, say, a soccer travel team that plays year-round, with practice sessions two or three times a week, plus games on the weekends and distant tournaments, it shouldn't come as a shock to you if she begins to view playing soccer more as a daily chore than as recreation.

Although there must have been isolated cases of burnout in athletes back in the 1950s and 1960s, the condition was most likely very rare. That's one major reason that parents of young athletes today (parents who are now in their late 30s to early 50s) have a difficult time trying to understand this phenomenon. The attitudes of those parents, who are eager to see their kids succeed in sports at the highest levels of competition — particularly on travel teams — tend to be ones of "How could any kid not enjoy playing sports? Heck, when I was a kid, I would have played sports all day long if my parents had let me . . . ."

In stark contrast, numerous psychological studies suggest that burnout among young athletes is a real and growing concern. Not surprisingly, many of these potential burnout athletes are members of travel, or highly competitive, youth league teams.

Kids today are exposed — at increasingly younger ages — to intense pressure and competition. And the direct message sent to kids is "Winning — and only winning — is the real key to not only success — but also to having fun." That is, the more you win, the more success you'll have, and thus the more fun you'll have.

Such an approach can be quite misleading to both child and parent. If a child isn't able to separate the two components — that is, if she begins to learn that you don't have any fun unless you win the game, you're planting the seeds for a potential case of burnout down the road.

The more fun your child has, the more success he'll enjoy. It's *not* the other way around. Fun is precisely what drove Michael Jordan. Certainly he's a diehard competitor, but his passion and the intrinsic enjoyment that he derived from the game of basketball as a kid and a teenager are what propelled him to great heights. The same is true for top athletes everywhere.

The Myth of "Staying Ahead of the Curve"

Despite the potential problems, enthusiastic sports parents today still want their kids to play on travel teams. They worry that, if the child doesn't make the travel team cut when he's 8 or 10 or 12, the child may not develop into a superb athlete. Parents seem fearful that their young athletes won't "stay ahead of the curve" — that they won't be considered among the chosen or selected few to go on to collegiate or professional stardom in sports.

Although it's easy to understand why you, as a concerned and loving parent, may feel personally disappointed if your young child doesn't make the cut on a travel team, you needn't lose too much sleep over it. Again, all sorts of top athletes weren't "good enough" to make a travel team when they were a kid. For example, two-time MVP of the WNBA, Cynthia Cooper, ran track as a kid. She didn't pick up a basketball until she was 16! And she certainly didn't compete on a travel team.

Chapter 5

Understanding the Differences between Individual and Team Sports

In This Chapter

▶ Coping with winning and losing in individual sports

▶ Dealing with your child's frustrations

▶ Finding and hiring a coach for your child

*W*hat if your child opts for a competitive sport such as tennis, golf, swimming, or wrestling — sports in which the individual athlete is in the spotlight. Are the pressures in those sports different?

Yes, they are. Even if your child shows every sign of becoming the next Tiger Woods or Martina Hingis, there are certain guidelines that, as a concerned sports parent, you have to be aware of. Assuming that your little one starts competing at a relatively tender age — around 5 or 6 — you have to understand certain assumptions about individual competition: Specifically, that your child will very quickly become aware of winning or losing in his sport. In fact, he'll become aware of winning and losing much sooner than the kids involved in team sports. And even more importantly, your individual athletic performer will become keenly aware that he is solely responsible for his victories or defeats.

Helping Your Child After an Individual Loss

Children who compete in team sports have less self-consciousness of having their individual egos on the line. A child can find solace in the group experience, as in: "Well, the team didn't play well today, but at least I did . . ." or "Yeah, I know our team lost, but it wasn't my fault — the coach told me I played well . . . ."

In other words, in a team sport like soccer, basketball, hockey, and the like, the youngster can more easily protect her fragile ego from a negative outcome of the game by simply distancing her performance from the others on the team. For little kids (and even some bigger kids), this form of team alibi can go a long way toward ensuring that the sports experience is fun.

However, contrast the *team* alibi with the situation of an *individual* athletic performer such as a tennis player, golfer, gymnast, or swimmer. Here, from the very first time they start to compete, youngsters learn right away that either you win or you lose.

There's rarely any middle ground, nor any opportunity to find an acceptable alibi to fall back on. At most, the individual athlete may claim, "The ref was terrible! He cost me the match!" or "I wasn't used to the tennis surface — and I wasn't feeling all that well today." But by and large, these alibis provide little solace to the young athlete and his or her efforts.

Even worse, if the youngster continues to not compete well, or not do as well as the parents expect, the child runs the risk of losing interest in the sport and turning away from it. After all, who wants to keep losing? No child enjoys, or accepts, that. (Chapter 3 has more tips on helping kids deal with disappointment in sports.)

Dealing with an "Alibi Ike"

So what do you do if your child becomes an "Alibi Ike" in her individual sports? For starters, try a little patience. It's one thing if your child is only 8 and complains that "the sun was in my eyes" or "the ref doesn't like me" or "the other player was cheating." For an 8-year-old child, such excuse-making, while not very pleasant, is a common psychological defense mechanism.

But by the time a child is 13 or older, such alibi-making is not acceptable. Ideally, by the time the child has reached this stage in his career, he will have learned that such behavior is totally unsportsmanlike. Worse yet, if he doesn't learn this essential lesson of sports, pretty soon he'll be making excuses about why he shouldn't be playing at all.

So in the early years, it's vital that you, as the parent, spend some time with your child and explain that when one competes in a sporting event, one may win or one may lose. Of course, in most cases, your little athlete will normally expect that she'll be the one who wins. But particularly in those competitions where there's going to be only one winner in, say, a field of 36 or 64 (such as a golf tournament or a gymnastics competition), this kind of parent-to-child conversation is essential.

Reinforcing that they can only do their best

Your children have to have a solid comprehension of what you truly expect from them — and that doesn't necessarily mean that they have to win. Explain to your kids that you want them to do their best — that's all anyone can ask of oneself. But doing your best doesn't necessarily always equate with winning! That's a very difficult concept for kids to understand, but you can introduce them to it early in life.

Try something like this: "Jessica, I know you're looking forward to this tennis tournament today, and it should be a lot of fun. But when playing in competitive sports, just keep this thought in the back of your mind: You can't control your opponent, and you can't control the outcome — but the one thing you can control is yourself and your effort. And when you're finished today, if you can honestly say to yourself that you did your best, well, that's all you can ever ask of yourself."

This script is important. Use it to guide your kids as they find their way in individual sporting events.

"But I'll never beat that other player!"

The notion that "I'll never beat that other player" reflects the youngster's concern that his opponent is *always* going to dominate him in this sport. Your child's concern calls for a different explanation, such as the following:

"Well, remember you're only 8 years old (or 10 or 12). Kids grow and develop at different rates and abilities. Right now, perhaps that other kid is a bit bigger than you, or stronger. But you have to understand that you're going to grow and change and get better as you get older — and if you continue to practice and work hard at your sport, the gap between you and your opponent is going to get smaller and smaller. But that's up to you and how much you want to work at your sport."

This kind of parental pep talk should be used when the child is beyond the sting of having lost the competition, and can finally sit down with you and listen to you carefully and unemotionally. Be careful *not* to promise that she's going to be the best someday (because you don't know that). But you can promise children that they will definitely get better, faster, stronger, and so on if they work hard at their skills.

Encouraging Sportsmanship in Individual Play

Sadly, here's a typical reaction to when a young athlete loses in an individual sporting competition:

The match ends, and your child, recognizing that he has lost, first throws his racquet on the ground, and then refuses to shake the victor's hand. He then runs off the court, finally bursting into tears.

This is, of course, a common experience with youngsters playing individual sports. It could be tennis, gymnastics, swimming, skiing, or any kind of sport. The problem is that the youngster who has just lost realizes that nobody is to blame for the loss except himself!

Even worse — and this may be more significant — the child is upset for losing today's competition, but deep down, he's even more upset because he realizes that his opponent is actually better at that sport than he is. Maybe it's because the opponent is bigger, or faster, or stronger, or more experienced, but for lots of young competitors, coping with the reality that one of their same-age peer competitors is better than they are in their chosen sport can be quite difficult.

As a parent, this kind of situation can be quite vexing. Here are a couple of suggestions on how to handle your child's disappointment delicately:

- ✔ "Son, I know it really hurts that you didn't do as well as you would have liked. But remember, if you're going to play sports, you're going to have to live by the rules of good sportsmanship. And that means — win or lose — you have to act in an appropriate manner. Otherwise, you run the serious risk of not being asked to play again."

- ✔ "Sometimes, it's not that you didn't win the competition — it's simply more a case that your opponent had a terrific day. That is, you didn't lose the match — the other player simply won it. Suppose Pete Sampras beats Andre Agassi in a tennis match. No one would say that Agassi "lost," but that Sampras was on top of his game that day."

I can't stress enough that young athletes have to learn these basic rules of sportsmanship while developing their other skills. If kids don't learn the rules of protocol early, or if the rules aren't enforced, there's a good chance that the youngsters may never learn good sportsmanship as they get older and compete at higher levels.

Kids who don't abide by the rules of sportsmanship find as they get older in their sports that while their athletic talents may be admired, they won't garner the same kind of overall respect as some of their more evenly-minded peers do. Even to this day, former tennis great John McEnroe, who was known throughout his career for his unnecessary and unsportsmanlike tantrums, is known more for his outrageous behavior than for his accomplishments on the court.

Finding the Right Coach for Your Individual Athlete

Many parents, eager to give their children a head start in an individualized sport, ask around to find a private coach or instructor to help their young athletes. Although in most cases this is a fine idea, bear in mind a few guidelines when looking to hire such a specialized coach:

- **Do your homework!** Don't go solely on the recommendations of others. Ask the prospective coach how he or she actually interacts and coaches the child. Be wary of those coaches who feel that their style is the *only* way to coach kids.

  Make a point of getting the names of other kids that the coach has worked with. Call the parents of those kids, find out what they think of the coach, and most importantly, find out why they are no longer working with that coach. And check the local police department to see if the coach is listed for any criminal or aberrant (child molestation) behavior. This may sound harsh, but cases of child molestation do happen all over the country.

- **Watch the coach in action with other kids.** See if you can actually watch some of the coach's protégés go through a session. See for yourself whether you like the way the coach puts each player through his paces.

- **Go over realistic goals.** Discuss with the coach what specific goals you have for your child — not in terms of long-range plans (like making the U.S. Olympic team), but rather, in terms of the aspects of your child's game that you want the coach to improve (for example, the child's footwork, stamina, shot, and so on). Write down these goals as specifically as possible and give the list to the coach.

- **See if the coach smiles.** Remember, it's still supposed to be fun. Be wary of the taskmaster who sees coaching the kid as a life-or-death proposition. In the long run, you want your child to keep playing the sport rather than quit because the coach is too tough.

> ✔ **See if your child and the coach build a rapport.** This part of the process, unfortunately, you really can't judge until your child has gone through several practice sessions with the coach. But your child will certainly be the first to tell you whether she gets along with the coach, and enjoys working with her.

If you start getting a strong sense that your youngster doesn't enjoy the practice sessions, or is coming up with reasons why he doesn't want to go to practice, these tip-offs may indicate that there's no real rapport being built between the two.

Coaching Your Own Child in Individual Sports

There's nothing inherently wrong or dangerous about coaching your own child in either an individual or team sport. In fact, if done properly and with the right amount of enthusiasm, it can be a wonderful shared experience for parent and child. However, there are hidden landmines along the way that you have to be careful with.

Understand that it's very difficult to draw a line between being a parent and a coach. That's a fine line to walk. Most youngsters will try to take more liberties with their own mom or dad who is their coach than with another grown-up who is working with them. The mere fact that a kid can call you "Mom" or "Dad" is indicative of the special bond your child has with you. And although you may not have any problem slipping from the role of "parent" to "coach," your child may find the distinction a lot more blurry.

If you want, you can try and delineate this difference for your child. Try this approach: Tell her that when you're on the tennis court, the golf course, or at swim practice with her, she ought to view you as her coach first and her parent second. Yes, of course, you still love her and want her to be happy, but if she wants to gain from your skills and experiences, this may be a productive way to go about improving in her sport.

This can be quite challenging for a child, so don't push the concept too strongly. If you find that she really has difficulty getting coached by you, find another coach for her.

All parents who serve as coaches run the risk of trying so hard to teach their youngsters how to perform better that they also run the risk of alienating their child. Tiger Woods, who was tutored from an early age by his dad, Earl, on how to play golf, clearly recalls that his dad never pushed him into playing or practicing. If Tiger ever told his Dad that he didn't want to play golf on a particular day, Earl would immediately back off and say, "Fine, that's okay with me." Perhaps this explains why Tiger has never shown any signs of "burning out" too early in his professional career.

Coaching your child also raises other complications as to how to provide constructive criticism. Above everything else, this is an area that can be quite tricky — for parent and child.

Part II
Coaching Tasks

The 5th Wave   By Rich Tennant

'We covered the basics today —
hitting the ball, tying our shoelaces
and why I have hair growing out of
my nose."

In this part . . .

This part covers the basics of becoming a youth coach. Whether you've never done it before or you're a seasoned veteran, all of the basic information you need is here, including how to put your priorities in order, how to prepare for the upcoming season, how to organize practice sessions, and how to plan for an actual game or meet.

You also can find lots of tips and scripts on how to ensure that your team has a pleasant experience by avoiding the common problems that many youth coaches encounter.

Chapter 6

Outlining Your Responsibilities As a Youth Coach

In This Chapter

▶ Checking first with your child

▶ Determining whether you should be the head coach or an assistant coach

▶ Teaching and enforcing a sense of discipline

▶ Working with the parents of your players

*V*ery few experiences in life can be as rewarding — or as frustrating — as being the coach for a youth sports team. The experience you have all depends on your approach.

Coaching (especially coaching young kids) is not as easy as you may think. You may be a diehard fan of the sport, know all the rules and strategies, and perhaps played the sport yourself when you were growing up. But simply being a fan, or having played the game doesn't qualify you as a coach to handle the emotional roller coaster of handling a youth team.

Certain traits, such as being sensitive to the individual needs of each player on your team and behaving as a responsible adult at all times, are absolutely essential. You also have to be calm, very patient, and also have a strong sense of understanding that you're dealing with kids — not professional athletes.

The truth is that any coach can learn the strategies and the Xs and Os of the game. The hard part is knowing how to get each and every kid on your team to want to go out and work hard during practice, and when game day comes, to go out and compete in the sport with overwhelming enthusiasm.

If, at the end of the day, you can look at your team and see a wide array of smiling faces, you know you've truly won as a coach — regardless of the final score of the game. That's what good coaching is all about — very few experiences in life are as wonderful as having a bunch of kids respond in a positive way to your coaching.

Thinking about Volunteering as a Coach

Should you coach? Assuming that you've gotten the go-ahead from your child (see the following section) *and* that you're ready to prepare yourself for the season, there are lots of reasons why you should take part.

✔ Being there with your child is fun. Talking about the team, the practice sessions, and the games is all part of having fun with your child. In addition, especially with little athletes, youth sports teams can be somewhat daunting at times — and it's reassuring for your child to know that you're there for him.

✔ You can have a positive impact not only on your own child's sports experience, but also on all the other kids' experiences as well.

✔ As the head coach or assistant, you can monitor all situations closely and make certain that all the adults act like grown-ups. Some youth league coaches can get carried away and lose their perspective when it comes to youth sports.

This monitoring is an important aspect of being involved in your child's team whether you coach or not. No doubt you have heard the horror stories of coaches using profanity at games, verbally attacking referees or umpires, pushing the kids to win at all costs, or playing only "favorite" kids. Sadly, this type of abominable behavior does occur. By helping out as a coach, you can do your part to make certain that these kinds of ugly coaching patterns don't take place.

Getting the green light from your child

Before you really start thinking about coaching your son or daughter's youth team, the first question to ask is the one directed at your child. Several months before the start of the season, you owe it to your child (regardless of his age) to see whether he would like you to either serve as the head coach or as an assistant coach.

I suggest this for two reasons:

✔ The youth sports experience is still about your child and how to bring him joy. Although most children are thrilled at the idea of having Mom or Dad serve as a coach, a few kids may prefer that the parents *not* coach their team. So first ascertain whether your child really wants you to coach. It should be *his* choice — not yours.

✔ If your child indicates that she would like you to coach her team, give yourself enough time to prepare for the upcoming season. That means figuring out — several weeks in advance — how to fit practices and games into your time schedule, how you can prepare for practices, and how you can bone up on the rules and strategies of the sport, and so on. In most cases, it also means that you need to contact the league board, which oversees the league, to make certain that they know you want to help out as a coach. Ask whether they have any information, seminars, videos, or other programs that can help you prepare for the role.

Determining whether you have the proper temperament

Do any of the following sound like you?

- Do you ever find yourself cursing out loud during the course of a kids' game?

- Is your voice hoarse after a game from yelling?

- Or maybe you find yourself so nervous that you're compelled to go off into the woods for a quick cigarette during halftime?

- Or maybe you blow up at the kids when they don't perform a drill properly, or they just aren't paying attention to what you're teaching?

- Or perhaps you brood for hours after a loss, and that loss ruins your weekend?

If any of this behavior sounds like you, don't coach kids. If you can't keep your emotions in check and your temperament is just not suited to the invariable ups and downs of coaching kids, then don't struggle against yourself or the kids on the team. Just don't do it.

Hey youth coaches, listen up!

Steve Sampson, head coach of the U.S. men's national soccer team, has the following tips:

- "If a coach is constantly talking or yelling at players during the game, it prevents your players from thinking for themselves.

- "Negative comments or over-coaching only discourages children from continuing to play soccer. The more our young soccer players enjoy themselves, the greater the likelihood that they will remain in the game.

- "Coaches of the youngest players must provide an environment where fun, not winning, is the main objective."

(Source: *Referee*, June, 1998).

If you still want to be involved with the team, perhaps you can help out by bringing juice and fruit to the games. Or you can help out as the timekeeper. You can help in lots of ways, even if coaching isn't suited to your personality.

And relax. Lots of people — even well-educated, morally upstanding, best-of-intentions folks fall into this category. Monday through Friday, they're wonderful parents and great people in the community. But come the weekend, somehow, their inner dark side emerges and they almost lose control of themselves when coaching kids.

Finding the time

Parents have many reasons why they don't volunteer to coach, such as:

- ✔ "Practices are held on Saturday mornings, and I like to sleep late on Saturday."
- ✔ "I never played the sport — I don't know the rules — how could I coach?"
- ✔ "I'm just too busy to coach kids."

There's an endless list of reasons why moms and dads don't coach. But just remember that if you don't help out, then you are, in effect, handing the coaching reins and responsibilities to some other parent — and your child may end up playing for a coach who makes the youth sports experience a nightmare for you and for your child. If coaching problems do erupt during the course of the season, then you have no one to blame except yourself for not volunteering and getting involved.

Do your best to find the time to help out in some capacity. Most sports seasons are fairly short (no more than 10 or 12 weeks), and the time passes quickly. Every youngster and their parents have every right to expect that the coach will do a fine job — and in most cases they do. But just in case, you can help pave the way for a fun season for all by finding the time to help out.

Head Coach or Assistant Coach?

Some parents assume that being an assistant coach is a lot less demanding than being the head coach. That's just not true.

Both jobs involve commitment, organizational skills, an even temperament, a desire to teach, and a careful sensitivity towards each child's needs, talents, and personality. Even though the head coach is ultimately responsible for the team's welfare, as an assistant coach, you should be there to help and aid the kids and the other coaches in any way you can.

✔ As head coach, you're in charge of organizing the team, both on and off the field. That means being in attendance at the pre-season league meetings, when the rosters, equipment, uniforms, rule book, and other essential items are handed out. It means contacting all the kids on the team (or the team parents) to let them know about the practice and game schedules, to make certain that they have directions to any away games, to let them know how to handle a game that may be postponed or called off because of inclement weather, and of course — knowing how to run the practice sessions and coach the games.

(If this all sounds daunting, relax. In Chapter 9, I give you tips to help you organize your plans and ensure that everybody on the team has fun, learns the game, and has a chance to play, then everybody goes home happy — both kids *and* their parents.)

✔ An assistant coach is on hand to help with all of the head coaching responsibilities, which may mean making phone calls, checking on directions, and so on. Most importantly, if the head coach can't make it to a practice session or a game, the assistant coach steps in and runs the program. In addition, the assistant coach acts as an extra set of eyes and ears for the head coach, making certain that all the kids are participating in the practices and games, and are enjoying themselves. It's an important — and vital — job.

Focusing on Your Top Priority As a Coach

To ensure that your kids have a great experience on your team — especially if you're coaching the younger ages (5 to 12) — always recall these two basic rules of coaching:

✔ Each kid wants to play in the game — and play a lot.

✔ Each kid's parents want to see him or her play — and play a lot — in the games.

Unfortunately, a gung-ho coach often misunderstands or simply doesn't accept these fundamental rules of coaching. In contrast, some coaches' general perception is that

✔ The kids and their parents want to win, and win a lot.

✔ My job as the coach is to make sure that our team wins.

You can see the problems that can crop up with this basic difference in philosophy:

- ✔ **The coach's perspective:** "I have an obligation to put forth the best team I can. And then, once we have a big lead, I can then give the better players a chance to take a breather and then I confidently put in my weaker kids. . . ."

- ✔ **The parent's perspective:** "The only thing I care about is seeing my kid play in the game, and play a lot. When she plays, she has fun. And she doesn't have fun when she's sitting out."

This one seemingly simple difference in perception accounts for all kinds of friction between parent and coach.

If you're the coach of a youth league team, make it your number one priority to ensure that all your players get a lot of playing time in each game. Your team may end up losing a few more games than you wanted to, but in the long run, everybody on your team will go home happy — not because they lost but because they all had a chance to play, and play a lot.

To help accomplish this goal, check with the league directors before the season to see if they can keep the number of players on each roster at a reasonable number. If, for example, you're coaching basketball, ask that each roster have only eight kids (five kids play at a time). That ensures that all of the kids get lots of playing time.

Other coaching priorities to consider

Besides having fun, you have other priorities to think about when coaching kids. Ranking them in terms of importance is difficult, but certainly you can impart several essential lessons to boys and girls in sports. (See Chapter 2 for ideas on what ages to teach these concepts during.) Those priorities include:

- ✔ **Sportsmanship:** Never assume the kids know what sportsmanship means. Teach it, show it, and enforce it.

- ✔ **Commitment:** Explain to youngsters their responsibility to be at practice and at the games, on time and every week.

- ✔ **Team play:** Introduce the basics of working towards a common goal as a team (for example, passing, defense, and praising one's teammates).

- ✔ **Conditioning:** Kids should learn early from their coach about being in shape and how to achieve that state.

- ✔ **Learning the rules:** Teach the rules of the game to the kids. Don't assume that they (or their parents) know them!

- ✔ **Helping them believe in themselves:** Playing sports and mastering athletic skills builds self esteem. And as the coach, you can help that child do just that simply by praising his skills, effort, and dedication to his task.

But what about winning?

The sense of winning and losing is a concept that should not be a top priority for you or the child in the early developmental years. Concerns about victories and defeats occur naturally as a child grows into the junior high school and high school years. In the beginning years (ages 5 to 8), most youth league teams don't even keep score — and quite frankly, you don't need to, either.

If the kids want to keep score among themselves, that's fine. But there's really nothing gained by having the parents keep a scoreboard, or league standings, or playoffs, or All-Star teams at any age younger than 10. After all, in the grand scheme of life, does it really make any difference who wins the third grade basketball championship in your town? (And if it does, then maybe you need to take a step back.)

You have other priorities to consider, but these certainly cover the basics. Use these as guidelines whenever you interact and communicate with the kids on the team.

Having fun

Many volunteer coaches assume that the top priority in the youth leagues is to win (and win all the time). These kinds of coaches fully believe that "The key to having fun is to have success!"

Unfortunately, too many youth coaches subscribe to this belief system and it doesn't work — at least with kids under the age of 13. The truth is, the key to having *success* is having *fun* — not the other way around.

No players cut, no playbooks, no whistles . . .

John Gagliardi has been the head football coach at St. John's University (Minnesota) for close to 50 years, and his Division III college football team boasts an overall record of 352-104-11. That's mighty impressive for a coach who has more college wins than Penn State's Joe Paterno or Florida State's Bobby Bowden.

Even more impressive is Coach Gagliardi's "revolutionary" philosophy of working with highly competitive college athletes. His program includes the following: no cuts, no staff meetings, no playbooks, no whistles in practice, no Gatorade celebrations after games, and so on. And by the way, he insists that the players call him "John" — not Coach.

Think about Coach — er, John — the next time you put together your own coaching philosophy.

(Source: *USA Today,* November 19, 1998)

Let the kids have fun. If the kids don't see games and practice sessions as fun and enjoyable, they quickly lose their enthusiasm for the sport — and for you. Making sure it's fun may mean some planning as well as some spontaneous moments from you, the coach. Practices in particular can become tedious, so feel free to add some fun days such as the following into the mix:

- ✔ Have a parents-kids game where the moms and dads play against the kids on the team.

- ✔ Plan a segment of practice where the kids have the freedom to practice anything they want.

- ✔ Hold a review session when they can "replay" their favorite plays from previous games (that is, they can re-enact their favorite plays, shots, passes, and so on).

Spontaneous fun is an instant cure-all for when practices become long and boring. Always have a couple of "spontaneous" sessions or games to add into your bag of coaching tricks.

Remembering That Young Athletes Are Not Professional Athletes

Hold onto your clipboards and write this one down: Kids are only professionals at being kids. Too many coaches make the mistake of assuming that kids are just smaller versions of professional athletes and as such, expect kids to perform in much the same way that the pros do.

Here are some of the admittedly unprofessional behaviors you can expect:

- ✔ **Kids make errors.** Lots and lots of them. They drop easy pop-ups; they strike out; they miss easy shots into the goal; they run the wrong way; they don't know the score.

- ✔ **Kids cry.** A lot. And even as they get older — around ages 12 to 14 — kids still cry. A lot. They still make errors, drop balls, miss easy shots, and at times, daydream out in the field.

- ✔ **Some kids like to pick daisies during the game or play in the dirt — while on the field.** They're just happy to be there and don't want to be yelled at.

- ✔ **Kids are supposed to be kids!** While you may be concerned about the final score and who was the team's leading scorer in the game, your kids may have been more impressed that it was a rainy day and that they were able to get their shiny new uniforms all dirty and muddy. That's one of the important aspects of having fun in sports that too many grown-up coaches forget.

No matter what level of kids you coach, sometimes your blood pressure rises, and your adrenaline pumps through your system because you're so emotionally involved in that game. But as an adult you can recognize when the competitive juices start flowing and still keep your act altogether on the sidelines.

If you discover that you can't do that, then you probably want to reevaluate continuing your role as coach and quietly step aside (see the "Determining whether you have the proper temperament" section, earlier in this chapter, for a checklist of warning signs that you're beyond the limits of your patience). After all, nobody benefits when the coach is out of control on the sidelines. It's great to coach your child's team in youth sports, but only as long as you can keep yourself on an even emotional keel. That's essential.

What the Kids Want from You

The players on your team may quickly come to expect certain coaching behaviors from you. Even the youngest child easily understands that, as the coach, you are due a certain amount of respect and authority in order to do your job properly. You can earn that respect by practicing the skills I outline in this chapter.

In short, they expect you to provide the following:

✔ **Leadership:** Little kids, both figuratively and literally, look up to adults. They just naturally assume that if you're coaching, you must know what you're doing. That's good. Let them continue to believe that — even if you have never coached before. Kids want to believe that they have the best coach around, and it's important for you to maintain that lofty status in their minds.

Be a strong leader around the kids. Do the right things on the field. Say the right things on the field. Praise them so that they'll want to work hard. Give them the opportunity to improve. In short, be their team leader. That means being there for them to offer help, guidance, and a shoulder to cry on when things aren't going that well. That's what good coaches do for the kids on their teams.

For example, you may run a warm-up lap with the kids at the start of practice. Then lead them in calisthenics. You can greet all the children by their first names, and do so with a smile. In contrast, the non-leader coach isn't always on time. He doesn't pay much attention to the kids. He just throws the equipment out on the field, sits back on the bench, and hopes that practice goes by quickly.

A word from the master

In the annals of coaching, former UCLA basketball coach John Wooden is considered by many to be the most respected coach who ever blew a whistle.

In a *New York Times* editorial, Wooden summarized his coaching style this way: "In my view, quiet confidence gets the best results. Leaders shouldn't do all the talking. Part of their job is to learn, through listening and observation."

John Wooden won ten NCAA titles as the head basketball coach at UCLA from 1948 to 1975.

(Source: *New York Times,* May 15, 1998)

✔ **Organization:** Being organized takes some pre-practice planning, but a little preparation goes a long way in terms of doing a good job as a coach. Assume that most practice sessions typically last an hour or an hour and a half. Just as a teacher puts together a daily lesson plan, a coach can do the same. Try to literally plan out each segment of the practice so that the kids go from one skill activity to the next, and so that there's never any waiting around, trying to figure out what to do next. (Chapter 8 helps you organize practices.)

Organization also means finding out who the team parent will be (usually a mom or dad who volunteers to help out), and then working with him or her to let the kids on the team know how you're going to handle everything from uniforms to game directions to rain-outs. As the coach, it's up to you to organize, plan ahead, and be involved. Don't assume the other parents will handle any of this — because they won't.

The kids expect all this to happen — they expect you, as the coach, to be in charge of all this. Just as they expect their teacher to teach in an organized way, they expect you to be an organized coach.

✔ **Praise:** Perhaps you grew up in a time and place where praise was given on the sports field very grudgingly, where your coaches were gruff, tough, and hard to please. You remember when that old Vince Lombardi concept "winning isn't everything — it's the only thing" (which he never actually said) prevailed.

If this is your style, Coach, it's time for your wake-up call. Social attitudes and kids have changed. Children today expect, want, and demand praise from their coaches and teachers. And they want praise all the time. The sooner you accept this new approach and start giving out praise to the kids on the team, the better you'll be accepted as a coach. Praise is the lubrication that keeps the kids' engines working hard and smooth. The more praise you give them for their efforts, the more effort they'll give you.

✔ **Teaching:** Clearly, there's a real parallel between coaching and teaching. Most kids want to please the coach in much the same way that they want to please their teachers. They want to learn new skills, practice winning strategies, and show off their talents for you. Each one will vie for your attention. And the sooner you can get to know them individually, learn their names, and find out what excites them to work hard, the sooner they'll respond to your coaching.

✔ **Discipline:** Believe it or not, kids actually crave discipline. That may come as something of a surprise to you, but youngsters come to practice fully expecting that the coach is going to set up some basic parameters of disciplinary behavior. Just as the teacher doesn't allow kids to speak without raising their hand first, you have to set the guidelines right away as to how you want the kids to behave.

Take the time to point out to them that you expect them to be on time for each practice and game, that you expect them to be quiet when you're speaking, and that you expect them to hustle and work hard. What to do if a child doesn't behave according to your rules? First, give her a warning. But if she misbehaves again, give her a "time-out." (That is, have her sit off by herself, away from practice but in sight, while you and the other kids continue to play.)

After a few minutes, the miscreant child will often begin to feel left out, and will want to return to action and rejoin her friends on the field. After 5 or 10 minutes, depending on the age of the young offender, ask the child to come back and join the others. But before she's allowed to come back, ask her first if she knows what she did wrong and whether she expects to do it again. Insist on this lesson; otherwise, the child may never learn the lesson of team discipline. (By the way, if the child misbehaves again, another time-out is given again.)

✔ **A sense of fair play:** As kids play more sports through their youth, they begin to expect that each contest will be played fairly. They'll fully expect that the other team isn't cheating, that the official or ref is calling an honest game, and that everything during the competition is equal for everyone.

As their coach, you can reinforce these expectations to make them come true. Remind the team that "fair play" is a major component of good sportsmanship, and that a win or victory that is achieved through cheating devalues the thrill of winning.

✔ **Kindness:** Be sensitive to each child on the team. Regardless of a child's athletic ability, he is there to enjoy himself, to have fun, and to play in the game. The young athletes count on you to make certain that they have those opportunities, regardless of the score of the game. If you look out for each and every kid on your team, then you're doing the best job you can, whether you win or lose.

What the Parents Want from You

Parents want you to make their child feel like they're something special.

Let each mom and dad know what a terrific young person their child is and acknowledge how hard their child works in practice. And let them know, of course, that you plan to give each child as much playing time as everybody else.

Oddly, and all too often, some youth coaches feel that it's their responsibility and obligation to openly inform parents that their children aren't doing well or don't put forth much effort in practice, and as such, their children won't play as much as the other kids because, quite frankly, their youngsters aren't very good. Such negative feedback is especially inappropriate with the parents of young athletes. As a coach, work with the parents to find out why their child isn't responding to your coaching style, and what you can do to make them more eager to practice and play in the games. In other words, work with the parents — not against them. Above all, you want to avoid conversations like the ones that follow.

The concerned parent of a 9-year-old approaches the soccer coach and asks politely why her child isn't getting a chance to play her favorite position. Whereas a sensitive coach may instinctively say, "Sure, Mrs. Smith, I'll make certain that I give Michelle more of a chance to play center forward in the next game," other less-savvy coaches may say something like:

> "I'd love to play Michelle more, but c'mon, Mrs. Smith, do you think it's fair to the other kids on the team if I put Michelle at center forward? I mean, the other girls on the team are trying to win these games, and let's face it, that really isn't her strongest position . . . ."

Or . . .

> "Look, Mrs. Smith, I'm not trying to be a bad guy, but let's face it — Michelle isn't ready yet to play a lot at center forward. I mean, suppose she plays there and does poorly. How is she going to feel about letting her teammates down?"

Or . . .

> "I'd love nothing more than to give Michelle a chance to play center forward but I'm afraid if I did, and the team didn't fare well, then I'd have a riot on my hands from the other parents. I mean, some of these other parents are nuts about winning all these games . . . ."

These responses sound terrible and they are. All of these so-called coaching "explanations" are ridiculous — and painful for the parents to hear. And yet, lots of youth coaches think that such responses are not only reasonable but downright kind. Make up your mind as to what kind of coach you want to be and then have the personal courage to stick to your convictions.

Chapter 7

Setting Up for the Season

. . . .

In This Chapter

▶ Understanding the rules of the game

▶ Preparing for that all-important first meeting with the team

▶ Letting parents know what you expect of them

▶ Working with your assistant coach(es)

. . . .

*A*fter you decide that you're going to serve either as a head coach or as an assistant for the upcoming season, your preparation starts well in advance of the first actual practice or game. Don't assume this preparation can wait until the last minute — it takes some time and commitment on your part. Especially if you haven't coached kids before or aren't that familiar with the sport, the more you prepare, the better off you'll be.

"But I've Never Coached Before!"

Even if you don't know a corner kick from a corner drugstore, or don't know the difference between a jump ball and a face-off, there's time to find out.

 As a coach, you need to take some time to brush up on the game, learn the lingo, get a sense of the strategies, and even find out about the game's history and its famous players. How do you do this? Simple. Go to a public library, go to the children's section, and check out a couple of books or videotapes on the sport you're going to coach. Or go to a local bookstore and purchase some books on the subject. Look for books (or videotapes) aimed at beginners (hint: many great sports books have ...*For Dummies* in the title!) because they are your best bet to learn about equipment, rules, fundamentals, skills, and so on. (Sharing a book with your own child is a wonderful way for the two of you to discover more about the sport — together.)

Regardless of whether you read the book with your son or daughter, however, make sure that you look upon your reading homework as a serious assignment. That way, when the coaches get together before the season to go over the teams and scheduling, you will be somewhat better informed about the coaching endeavor you're involved in. Recognize that many beginning coaches become quickly intimidated when they realize that they aren't as "prepared" or as "experienced" as the other coaches. But beginning coaches who take their homework more seriously than the other coaches are often more conscientious in their task. That's a plus for you!

It's still up to you to find the time to make this work. Whether you're the head coach or an assistant, you gotta learn the rules.

Learning the Rules of the Game — and of the League!

When you teach the rules of the game to the kids on your team, be certain that you explain the rules in a manner that is age-specific for the children. In other words, make the rules simple to understand. In addition, go easy on the Xs and Os of game strategy — you're not teaching advanced calculus here! You're teaching the basics to a bunch of little kids. (Flip to Chapter 2 for an idea of which topics are appropriate for which ages.) The kids will quickly pick up on the rules of the sport, and before you know it, both the kids and their parents may bombard you with questions about the technical rules of the game.

- ✔ "Coach, aren't the kids supposed to rotate through every position on the field?"
- ✔ "Coach, my kid has earrings that can't be removed easily — but she can still play in the game, right?"
- ✔ "Coach, can you explain the infield fly rule to my 8-year-old?"
- ✔ "Hey, Coach, what's the rule about high-sticking in hockey? Is that a minor or a major penalty in this league?"

To be prepared to answer these kinds of questions, make it your business to track down the league commissioner several weeks before the season begins, and get a written copy of the rules and regulations for your team. Then, after you have the rules and regulations, study them!

Even if you played the sport yourself as a child or follow the game closely today, you still have coaching homework to do. Bear in mind that many of the rules you know as a fan of the professional or collegiate game may not be the same rules that are used at the youth level. For example, just because you know that the offside rule is a critically important part of World Cup soccer, you may be surprised to discover that with younger children, the offside rule may not be observed or enforced in your soccer league. Or that youth soccer uses a smaller soccer ball than a regulation size ball. Or that the youth soccer field is smaller, and that kids play with only eight players on a team instead of 11.

These are precisely the kinds of playing rules you must be familiar with; otherwise, you run the risk of making some serious mistakes during the course of the season. Too many coaches assume that the rules are simple and straightforward. Many times they are not. Take the time now to learn them, and if you have questions, directly ask the league commissioner rather than a neighbor or another parent who coached last year.

For example, say you're coaching a youth league baseball team. Especially with kids under the age of 9, you may find all sorts of modifications to the rules being used in the games. The bases are closer, sometimes a parent or the umpire pitches instead of a child, only a certain kind of baseball can be used, and the batting order may allow for all the kids to hit rather than just the usual nine or ten players. If you aren't familiar with these rules — and dozens just like them — you could really find yourself in a tough predicament as the season gets underway. And as a coach, it is your job to know all these rules of the youth game before the very first pitch is thrown.

Don't forget the safety rules!

Every youth sports league has its own rules regarding safety equipment, so you need to know and enforce these safety rules. For example, in youth soccer, every child must wear league-approved shin guards. The soccer shoes also have to fit well and have the right kind of rubber spikes on the soles. And in most leagues, no jewelry is allowed.

The "no jewelry" rule can pose problems if a child has an earring or two that can't be removed easily. This is just the kind of question to ask the league commissioner before the season begins. In many leagues, a child is allowed to play if he or she affixes a bandage over each earring. But some leagues don't make

this exception. If you find out about this rule — and other safety regulations — before the season begins, you can let the parents know how to dress their children safely before the games start.

In most cases, the league can provide you with a written list of safety rules regarding equipment, and before each game, the referee (or official or umpire) will check to make sure that each player is wearing the correct equipment. In most cases, if the child is not wearing the necessary equipment (perhaps a mouth guard, shin guards, protective cup, or whatever), the official rightly will not allow the child to play until he or she dons the correct equipment.

In addition, make certain that all the kids and their parents know about the proper equipment they need in order to play in the league. You may want to write down the league rules regarding equipment and make copies to give to all the parents so that no one misunderstands the rules regarding equipment. Make every effort to emphasize that this is the parent's responsibility — not the coach's — and that a child who isn't properly suited up probably won't be allowed to play. That's not to punish the child, but to protect him or her from getting hurt.

Scheduling the All-Important First Team Meeting

Undoubtedly, the most important team meeting is the very first one of the year. You want both the kids and their parents to attend this meeting. To accomplish this, let them know that it's mandatory that they be there. Just to make sure that they get the message, send them a note in the mail, and then call them a week or two later to remind them of how important the first meeting is.

Be sure to emphasize *mandatory*.

Regardless of the age of the kids, the first meeting is important because it allows you to set the stage and the tone for the rest of the season. You get a chance to introduce yourself and your coaching philosophy to the players and their parents. The meeting should last no more than 20 to 30 minutes, and if you want, you can even hold a brief practice session afterwards. To stay on schedule, come with an outline of the items you want to cover in the meeting.

 ✔ **Have all the essential information already typed out and ready to hand out.** Essential information includes your name and home phone number, as well as the assistant coaches' names and numbers. If you have a team parent already, this is a good time to introduce him or her. Of course, you want his or her name and number on the sheet as well.

 ✔ **Find out who can help you.** If you haven't found a team parent yet (a team parent helps out with making phone calls in case of bad weather, getting travel directions, bringing juice/water to games, and so on), this is the perfect time to ask for a volunteer. Make sure that somebody steps forward — having a team parent will become invaluable to you. (If no parent does step forward, feel free to ask one of the more reliable parents to help you out.) And after you have this team parent in place, make sure that he or she understands how important that job is. Remember, the better your team parent, the easier your coaching job will become.

✔ **Explain the league rules of participation.** Let all the parents know if there are any mandatory rules regarding how much of each game every child must play. Let the parents know that you fully expect to abide by those rules, unless there are extenuating circumstances (such as a child missing several practices or games). Yes, we want the children to win, but "we're going to win according to the league rules. That's the way I coach." Above all, be firm in your philosophy. After all, you're the coach.

This is an important point to make because most youth teams usually have more players to the roster than can play at once. For example, if it's a soccer team, you may have 15 or 16 kids on the team whereas only 11 play at a time. If it's baseball, you may have 14 or 15 kids on your team when only 9 or 10 can play at one time.

Parents are sensitive to this reality, and they want to be openly reassured that their child is going to play in each game in accordance with the league rules regarding mandatory participation. That's why you have to know the league rules before this first meeting, and also why it's the first item to bring up in the team meeting with the parents in attendance.

✔ **Explain the rules regarding equipment and safety instructions.** This is of vital importance. Even though this may take a few minutes, you want to address this essential topic in this first meeting. Read out slowly and distinctly to everybody in attendance what the league stipulates regarding equipment. If no jewelry is allowed with no exceptions, make that clear to everyone. If the league forbids metal spikes, make that clear. If every player needs to have a mouth guard in place when playing, make that clear. If each player needs to wear a protective cup, again, make that clear.

In effect, you're trying to wipe away any misunderstandings or confusion that may come up during the rest of the season. Because all the parents and the kids are at this meeting, you can remind a parent during the season, "Remember how I explained that safety issue at the first meeting? The league rules are specific that your child can't play if he's wearing metal spikes instead of rubber ones. The metal spikes are more dangerous. That's not my rule, it's the league's rule."

Sounds simple, doesn't it? But you'll be surprised at how many times during the season these kinds of situations can pop up:

- "Coach, my daughter left her mouth guard home. She can still play today, can't she?"

- "Coach, my son doesn't like wearing his protective cup when playing hockey. He can still play without one, can't he?"

✔ **Ask the parents to review with you any medical concerns regarding their children in a private conversation, perhaps even after the meeting.** Medical information is just as important as the safety equipment issue! Because many parents would prefer to discuss this personal matter with you in confidence rather than in public, give them that option. For example, if a child has asthma and needs to use an inhaler, you as the coach need to know this. If another child has diabetes, it would be a great help for you to know this as well. If a child has a hearing problem, again, understanding that can help you coach her better. This same advice applies to any lingering or healing injuries that a child on the team may have. But remember, a medical condition is a personal issue to be discussed solely between the parent (and sometimes the child) and the coach. Respect the child's and the parent's wishes on these matters.

✔ **Discuss candidly with the moms and dads what you expect from them, especially with regard to their conduct at practices and games.** Naturally, you expect them to behave as mature adults and as positive role models in good sportsmanship for the kids. Sometimes during the games, they may feel tempted to call out to their kids, to criticize the ref, or to make ill-tempered remarks to the other team and their coach. But make clear to the parents that you don't want to hear any of that.

If they feel compelled to yell and scream on the sidelines, urge them only to offer praise and positive comments. Let them know that under league rules and under your own coaching philosophy, you simply will not tolerate any outrageous or unsportsmanlike behavior coming from the parents. Be firm and strong when announcing this. Tell them that there won't be any exceptions to this rule, and that you truly don't anticipate any problems with this. But if problems arise, the misbehaving parents will be asked to leave the game.

✔ **Talk about sportsmanship and how you expect the kids to behave.** Using examples, explain to the kids what it means to play in a sportsmanlike manner (shaking hands with opponents after the game, treating the officials with respect, no trash talking or taunting, and so on). Understanding and abiding by the rules of sportsmanship is not only essential, but it allows the kids to truly enjoy the spirit of competition. As such, let the youngsters and parents know that if they *don't* abide by these basic rules of sportsmanship, then they will find themselves on the sidelines during the game. They simply will forfeit their playing time. Again, be firm in your approach here. Remind the parents and the players that these are not difficult rules to live by — but if they have problems, the time to discuss them is now.

✔ **Go over team discipline briefly.** This tends to be something of a broad topic, and you don't want to get bogged down here or give the kids a list of disciplinary rules. They won't take notes, nor will they be able to remember too many rules. For the time being, just tell the kids and their parents that you expect them to be on time, to come to the practices, and if they can't make it to a practice or game for any reason, to contact you via telephone — ideally at least 24 hours ahead of time. Ask them *not* to simply tell a friend on the team to tell you that they're not coming to practice or a game. That's not fair. For the purposes of this short meeting, just let them know that you appreciate their willingness to commit to the team, and that this discipline becomes even more important as the season gets underway, so there will be consequences if a certain number of practices or games are missed.

Of course, sometimes conflicts arise, and then your coaching common sense comes into play. For example, a parent may come to you and explain that Emily can't make it to all the Saturday morning practice sessions because she has religious instruction at the same time as practice. That's a different kind of request from that of the parent who explains to you that her Samantha can't make it to all the Saturday morning practices because she has a hard time getting up on the weekends. As the coach, you have to draw a line as to what is an acceptable reason to miss practice and what isn't. Let the parents know at the first meeting that if they have a specific concern that involves their kids, it's always preferable to let you know well in advance so that you can make proper adjustments.

✔ **At the end of the meeting, take a few minutes to hand out schedules, directions to away games, and uniforms (make sure that the kids try them on and that they fit before they leave!).** In addition, take some time to meet and greet the parents you don't know. Try to learn each child's first name and introduce yourself to each one.

As you wrap up that first meeting, take a moment to ask for questions from the parents. This gives parents a golden opportunity to clear up any potential misunderstandings or misconceptions about what it is you want from them and their children during the course of the season. Surprisingly, even if you thought you were absolutely clear about your team policies, many parents still ask the same questions.

This is also the time when individual parents may come up to you with questions and requests. If you feel that the meeting is going on too long because you're being bombarded at this time with too many questions, simply ask the parent to call you at your home later. That way, you don't feel compelled to make snap decisions that may come back to haunt you later in the season.

Don't forget to smile throughout the meeting! This may sound silly, but if you come across as a tyrannical coach in your first meeting with the kids and the parents, they're not going to look upon the upcoming season as a fun experience. So just relax and smile. You're not trying to win the Super Bowl here — you're just trying to let the kids go out, have fun, and learn something about the sport. It's supposed to be fun — and as the coach, you're the one who sets the tone.

Working with Your Assistant Coach (es)

If you're the head coach of the team, it's always a good idea to call your assistant coach or coaches well in advance of that first team meeting. Ideally, if you don't know the individuals who have volunteered to serve as your assistants, it's a good idea to meet them in person rather than just say hello over the phone.

But after you've met, find out what kind of background your assistants have in coaching kids in this age bracket as well as their backgrounds in the sport. You're not asking for a resume here, but it can be a big help if it turns out that one of your assistants has some direct experience with a particular skill in the sport you're coaching. Suppose, for example, that your assistant coach used to be a goalkeeper in soccer. He'll be of great help to you in working with the kids who play that position. Or perhaps one of your assistant coaches has training as a paramedic. That's reassuring to know just in case some emergency medical help is needed during a practice or a game.

Beyond that, present yourself as the head coach, and as such, let your assistant coaches know your philosophy on coaching the team. Primarily, tell them that you expect to play according to the league rules, and that you want their help to do just that. You also want to point out to your assistant how important it is for her to serve as your "extra set of eyes and ears" in order to make certain that the kids don't get into trouble behind your back, that kids aren't teasing other kids, and that all of the kids are paying attention to what's happening on the field. As good a head coach as you may be, your job will be easier with an assistant or two working with you.

Also, forewarn your assistant that many times the assistant coach becomes the sounding board for or buffer between an upset parent and the head coach. The aggrieved mom or dad may complain to your assistant, not directly to you, in the hope that the assistant coach can better present their concerns. Usually, these concerns revolve around Billy not getting a chance to play a more desired position, or not getting enough playing time, or that even another player is being a "ball hog" and not passing the ball to their kids.

When situations like this happen — and they will — let your assistant coach know your preferences on how to handle it. Ask him to try the following technique:

1. **Listen to the parent for a good five or ten minutes. Let the parent have her say.**

2. **Don't try to defend the situation. Just tell the parent that you have heard her out, and that you — as the assistant coach — will definitely bring this to the head coach's attention.**

3. Bring the problem to my attention as soon as appropriate so we can discuss what to do.

Beyond helping you with that kind of parental problem, encourage your assistant coaches to behave in an appropriate manner themselves during the games. Remind them that they, too, are supposed to follow the rules of sportsmanship at all times and be a role model for the kids and the other parents. This is an important aspect of their being a coach.

Finally, remind your assistant coach that if, for some reason, you can't be at a practice or game, she should be ready, willing, and able to step up and pinch hit for you. If this situation occurs, be sure to let the assistant know in plenty of time so that she can prepare.

Chapter 8

Preparing and Conducting Practices

In This Chapter

- Planning and organizing a practice session
- Coaching efficiently and effectively in practice
- Dealing with disruptive behavior
- Dealing with alibis

One unspoken fear that holds many parents back from volunteering to coach youngsters is uncertainty about how to organize and run an efficient practice session for kids. That's a shame, too, because putting together a crackerjack practice for kids in any sport needs only the following ingredients:

- Preparing in advance
- Managing the practice time
- Coaching by walking around
- Planning "spontaneous" drills during practices
- Having fun

Preparing in Advance

Whether you're coaching the local swim team, a soccer club, or a peewee basketball team, an efficient and productive practice session starts with your preparation to ensure that the practice is worthwhile. Nothing is more boring or nonproductive than a practice session in which the coach simply stands around, circles the kids together, and says, "Okay, gang, what do you want to do today?" That's a sure sign that the coach isn't prepared.

Instead, prepare for your practice using the following steps:

1. **Several days before your practice session, take out a sheet of paper and a pencil.**

2. **Think about the last game the team played, or if they haven't played a game yet, determine in your mind which basic skills they have to develop in order to improve.**

3. **Jot down a quick list of those skills and drills you want to cover.**

4. **Keep in mind your total practice time available, and then block out 5-, 10-, or 15-minute blocks of time for each drill.**

5. **From there, start mapping out the order of your practice session.**

For example, assume that you have practice on Saturday morning, and the practice time lasts for one hour and 15 minutes, or a total of 75 minutes. You have chosen six skills to cover. Spending 15 minutes on each skill will take 15 minutes more than you have. If you allow 15 minutes for three drills and 10 minutes for the other three, you allow no time for rest in between. A more realistic plan may be to practice only 5 skills or to spend only 10 minutes on each skill so that the kids can take breathers and you can conduct some team business.

Dividing your practice sessions into regimented segments or blocks of time allows you to keep to your schedule. It also ensures that the team works on all the drills they need to, and keeps the action moving along at a brisk pace. Be sure to bring a watch with you to every practice!

Here's a sample practice schedule for a youth basketball team:

First 5 minutes:	Two laps and simple calisthenics to stretch and loosen up.
Next 5 minutes:	A quick review of what the team did well and not so well last game. Always talk about the team — never an individual player.
Next 5 minutes:	A simple drill, perhaps a line of lay-ups.
Next 5 minutes:	Work on defensive stance and lateral movement.
Next 10 minutes:	Work on rebounding, how to box out opponents.
Next 10 minutes:	Work on free-throw shooting.
Next 10 minutes:	Passing drills, how to hit the open player.
Next 10 minutes:	Running offensive plays, teaching basic give-and-go.
Last 15 minutes:	Controlled scrimmage.
75 minutes:	**Total practice time**

This simple act of thinking ahead about what the team has to work on makes each practice run smoothly and gives the kids a solid sense of progress toward their goals. Even better, when the session ends, you walk away with the self-satisfaction that your outline worked and that the action moved quickly. (Of course, occasionally you may want to veer away from your organized practice — I cover that subject in the "Developing a Sense of Spontaneity" section, later in this chapter.)

Getting Kids to Manage Their Time

You may already know how important it is to plan each activity in practice. Time management is not just important to you, however; it's important for the kids to learn as well.

✔ **Get the kids (and their parents) in the habit of arriving a few minutes early to each practice or game.** In many communities, several different teams use the same practice facilities, so you don't want to waste any of your allotted practice time. Remind the kids that if the practice session starts at 10 a.m., they should try to be there at 9:50 so that practice can start exactly on time. Always start practice right on time. If kids are late or straggle in, let them catch up to the rest of the team. Don't get in the habit of waiting for them — that's not fair to the other kids who are on time. Let the stragglers learn about being punctual from their friends — they'll get the message.

✔ **During a practice session, keep the kids constantly involved in the drills.** If you discover that you have too many kids waiting in line to do a drill, immediately break the one long line into two lines (or have your assistant coach do so). As long as they're involved and moving, kids of all ages will sense that they're making progress.

This strategy places some pressure on you to make sure that your drills and exercises maximize the kids' involvement. If you're not familiar with the sport's basic drills, go to the library, find a beginner's text about how to play the sport, take notes, and then, most importantly, go out and try some of these recommended drills yourself. Only by trying them can you get a better sense of just how difficult these drills are and how much time they require to perform. Structure the difficulty of the drills according to the age group and ability of your team.

If your practice drills take too much time in your practice sessions, try either shortening the amount of time that you devote to each drill or breaking up the drills for different practice sessions. Using a basketball example, if you don't have enough time to work on rebounding skills, just move that drill to the next practice. Use common sense: Work on those parts of the kids' game that they need the most help with.

Coaching by Walking Around

Managing by walking around is a well-accepted business practice. Top executives and managers know that to inspire subordinates to become more productive, work harder, and pay more attention to the job at hand, the boss has to get out from behind his or her desk and literally walk around the office or shop and interact with the workers. Even more important, the boss needs to chat with each employee, address employees by name, and get to know them on a somewhat personal basis. Making eye contact and spending some time with each worker makes a big difference in motivation.

That personalized touch of management by walking around works wonders, and it can work wonders for you, too, when coaching a bunch of kids. First, it's an excellent way of building rapport with each child. By using first names and offering a bit of praise during practice, you make each child feel special. Because you, the coach, make the time to talk to a kid individually, say something positive about him and his effort, and make eye contact with him, the child feels that he's special and that you're recognizing him as an important part of the team.

Developing a Sense of Spontaneity

Besides knowing how to plan ahead, you also need to know when to allow a little spontaneous fun to break into the action. Although it's important to have each practice mapped out, you have to balance your approach and give the kids a little time and space to be, well, kids.

For example, suppose the field is a bit wet and muddy from a rainstorm the night before. The kids on your soccer team are obviously enjoying getting a little dirty and muddy as they prance through the puddles. If you can see that they're having fun (hint: Are they laughing out loud?), feel free to set up a spontaneous "drill" that allows them to jump through the puddles. You may even design a competition to see which of the kids makes the biggest splash as they run through their drills.

Other spontaneous drills may include allowing the kids to play different positions from where they normally play during practice, allowing them to make up their own drills to practice, or even having a contest to see which member of the team can come up with the goofiest calisthenics exercise.

Moments like these are vital to keep the team laughing, to share a sense of team camaraderie, and to let them blow off some steam. And remember — because the kids take their behavioral cues from you and the other coaches, you need to join in the fun, too, and let the kids see you smile.

HEADS UP

Knowing what they don't know

Always assume that the kids on the team know nothing about the game. That is, they don't know about the rules of the game, or how to dress properly in the uniform, or what's the right way to behave in a game, or how to hustle.

Especially with younger kids, normally assume that they don't know. After all, the younger the children, the more chance that they have never played on a team before, and as such, they really don't know how to dress for a game, whether they should bring a water bottle for practice, whether they should bring a sweat-shirt in case it's cold, if they know how to get to the field, what's the best equipment to buy (and where), and so on.

Although some of these issues may seem quite obvious to your players, a few kids on the team often *don't* know and are usually too embar-rassed or inexperienced to ask for help or an explanation. So rather than leave anything open for misinterpretation, take the time to explain it all to the team.

Addressing Disciplinary Problems during Practice

Few coaches are spared from encountering some disciplinary problems during the course of a youth sports season.

EXAMPLE

- ✔ You're in the middle of giving your team some brief instructions when you notice that two of the ten-year-olds are holding their own conversa-tion and not paying attention to you.

- ✔ The team is working hard, except for one of the better players, who doesn't put forth much of an effort at all; in fact, he's even distracting some of the other kids with his shenanigans.

- ✔ It has become apparent that some of the older players on your team are teasing one of the younger kids, and they're being quite mean and per-sistent about it.

- ✔ One feisty 11-year-old on your team thinks that it's cool to swear and use curse words whenever she can — especially during practice sessions.

These are just some of the more common disciplinary situations that can occur when you're running practice. The key to handling these incidents is not to expect that they won't happen (because disciplinary problems almost always take place), but in knowing how to respond to them appropriately.

Setting the tone

You set the tone for discipline. Just like a teacher in a classroom, if you allow the children to be lax in their approach to practice and in their behavior, you're inviting trouble. You have to walk a fine line between being a warm and caring coach and letting the kids know that those who misbehave aren't going to be tolerated. Try this approach when you talk to the team:

"Kids, we're here to practice — and practice hard. We have only an hour to work on our skills, and we're going to move fast. If I have to stop to discipline you for goofing off, for not paying attention, or for not putting forth a solid effort, the entire team suffers because of it. Please, if you don't understand what I'm saying, let's talk about it now, because once we start, if you can't follow this simple rule, we'll have to let you sit out until you can. Now, does everybody understand? Good — let's go to work."

Drafting a code of conduct

Some coaches hand out a one-page code of conduct for the kids on the team to read and sign before the season begins. This code of conduct stipulates that if a child is to play on the team, he or she agrees to play hard, play by the rules, and not be disruptive during practices and games. The child then signs the code of conduct agreement, along with his or her parents.

The theory behind this written agreement is that it requires the children to focus directly on their behavior for the upcoming season and makes them aware that you will not tolerate unwanted or undisciplined behavior. Codes of conduct are much more common with older teams (such as junior high school or high school squads), but travel teams may use them also (see Chapter 4). They're less common with teams for kids under the age of 12.

If you suspect that discipline may pose a problem for the kids on your team, consider putting together a code of conduct agreement. If nothing else, you can use it as an important document in case one of the kids begins to misbehave during the season and you have to sit her out for a good portion of the game. When the child (or the child's parents) begins to complain, you can remind her (and them) of the code of conduct — an agreement everyone signed.

What is an appropriate punishment?

Although there is no one correct answer, the most acceptable form of "punishment" is to simply stop the practice, isolate the child who is causing the problem, and give him a "time-out." That means having him sit off to the side of practice and making him watch the action for several minutes.

Some coaches have other forms of punishment. Some prefer to have the misbehaving child run extra laps. Other coaches may scream, yell, or try to verbally embarrass the child. And some youth coaches just ignore disruptive behavior as best they can and try to work around it.

These approaches — running laps, being yelled at, or being ignored — have been around for years. Although these traditional responses to a discipline problem may be common, the truth is that they aren't very effective. In most cases, the kids either just don't pay attention to what you're yelling about or in the case of running laps as a punishment, after completing the chore, quickly forget about it. Neither approach achieves the desired effect.

When you single out a child for non-cooperative behavior and tell her to take a time-out and sit out of the fun, this ostracizing maneuver gets the kid's attention right away and also goes a long way in letting her know that you do not tolerate disruptive behavior. First, the miscreant is embarrassed simply because she's been singled out (in a negative light) by the coach. That's bad enough. But then, after a few minutes of sitting out and watching her friends enjoy themselves during the practice session, it's the rare child who doesn't feel the immediate desire to rejoin them right away. Above everything else, kids like to play — both in practice sessions and especially in games.

Although this time-out strategy is a good one, like anything else, it can be overused. Try to reserve it for the most disruptive behaviors. Even though kids occasionally chatter a bit amongst themselves in practice and sometimes let their attention drift away from the action, remember that kids have relatively short attention spans, and you need to adapt to theirs, not the other way around. That's why you want to keep the action in practice always moving.

Furthermore, if you do order a child to the sidelines, be careful not to let the child sit out for more than five minutes. Then, to make sure that she understands why the behavior was wrong, quietly find your way over to the sidelines and address the child, gently, face-to-face:

"Sara, do you understand why I made you sit out? Do you understand that we're not going to tolerate any disruptive behavior on this team? Good. Okay, now, get back in there and let's go to work."

Be firm, but gentle and direct, in your approach. Remember, the only real power that any coach has over his or her team is playing time. Because you decide who plays in each game and in practice, that's the ultimate power — and the kids (and their parents) know that.

Using your coaching "common sense"

No matter how much preparation you do, you'll have to use your common sense. If a situation is brought to your attention that isn't covered by the league rule book or even by the scope of this book, you're going to have to rely on your own adult judgment.

You have two children who are always picking on each other during the practice sessions and before games. Their ongoing behavior has become a real concern to you and a distraction to the other players. Do you simply sit them down and talk to them? Do you threaten them with reduced playing time? Do you make them run extra laps? Or do you call their parents and explain to them that you're having a real problem here?

There is, as you may suspect, no correct answer here. You have too many factors to take into consideration; each situation and each child is totally different. Because you have seen the problem firsthand, you have to reflect on the situation, talk it over with your assistant coach, and then make your decision. But your decision has to be well thought out, sensitive to all parties concerned, and fair in terms of any punishment that you hand out.

Team disciplinary decisions are hard for any coach to handle. But regardless of the situation, keep in mind that ultimately, as the head coach, it's your call. As long as you have given the matter serious thought and have done your homework, your decision will be respected, even though everyone involved may not like it. As a coach, even in a youth league, respect still comes before popularity.

Dealing with a Child Who's a Chronic Discipline Problem

You may have a child on your team who doesn't respond to your repeated directives about disciplined behavior. Even worse, the time-outs you give him for disruptive behavior really don't have much impact on him.

If the situation has reached a point where you feel that the child isn't responding to you at all, call the child's parents and ask to speak to them about this problem. Be very, very careful in how you approach this conversation, because quite understandably, most parents are instinctively protective of their kids, are defensive, and don't want to hear any kind of bad news about their child from a volunteer youth coach. The situation can become even more complicated if the parents are friends or neighbors of yours; after all, how would you like it if a neighbor came to you and told you about a problem she was having with your child?

Because of these very real concerns, you have to be quite diplomatic. Perhaps you think it's not worth the effort or hassle to even have this conversation with the child's parents. But on the other hand, is it fair to all the other kids on the team if a child who routinely is disruptive and refuses to play by the rules of discipline ruins their fun and enjoyment? Remember that you have an obligation to all the children and their parents.

I generally suggest that instead of coming straight out and complaining to the parents that their child is a pain in the neck and asking what they are going to do about it, try a more subtle, sensitive approach that emphasizes *cooperation* rather than confrontation. Here's a sample telephone conversation:

> "Hello, Mrs. Jones? Hi, this is Rick Wolff. I'm the coach of Mike's soccer team. Say, Mrs. Jones, it's pretty obvious that Mike loves to play soccer — he has tremendous energy and I know he enjoys being on the team — but I was wondering if you could help me with a little problem I'm having."

This introduction lets the parent know that you acknowledge that Mike loves playing the game and is enthusiastic. Every parent wants to hear that about her son or daughter. But then, you hint gently that you're having a problem and need her advice.

> "You see, Mrs. Jones, I try to run a fairly organized practice session each Saturday for all the kids, and well, we try really hard to keep the kids moving and having fun during practice. But I've noticed that Mike occasionally has had some concerns in practice."

Stop here and pause. Invariably, the parent will ask, "Concerns? What kinds of concerns?"

> "Well, that's where I thought you could help me. You see, sometimes, when we have the kids do some basic calisthenics, Mike doesn't join in, or if we do some kicking drills, he either doesn't want to participate or he just doesn't try very hard, and occasionally he actually interferes with the other kids on the team who are trying to work hard. You see, Mrs. Jones, I don't want to dampen the boy's enthusiasm for the sport, but if all the other kids are doing the drills and working hard, I really don't know what's the best approach for Mike."

Again, pause here. Let the parent digest what you're saying and see how she responds. Most of the time, if there really is a problem that is bothering the child, the parent can talk to him and find out why he doesn't like to behave in practice, and then ideally, relay that information back to you.

But the bottom line is that you've told the parent what the problem is, and that you're looking for cooperative guidance from them. You should also add:

"Y'know, Mrs. Jones, I've even had to give Mike several time-outs during practice sessions, which I really don't want to do, but the kids know the rules and if they misbehave, they have to have a time-out."

Very calmly, you've told the parent that the discipline problem has reached a point where something has to be done. At this juncture in the conversation, once again, you should stop and wait for the parent to respond. More times than not, she shares your concerns about this problem, and is glad to offer some suggestions as to how you can handle the child.

However, sometimes your phone call is greeted not with parental concern, but with outright anger. Always keep in mind that most moms and dads are not objective about their kid's behavior, and they are honestly stunned to hear that their little angel has become a bit of a problem for you. This kind of parent becomes instinctively defensive and usually totally denies that his child poses a problem. In fact, the parent may even tell you something like the following:

"There's nothing wrong with my kid — the real problem with the team is you — you're a lousy coach! My kid is angry and sulks in practice because he wants to play center forward and you keep playing him on defense. That's why he doesn't pay attention to you — and quite frankly, I can't blame him!"

If this should happen, although you'd probably like to argue back, whatever you do — don't lose your temper! Realize that you're dealing with an emotional parent who doesn't want to hear any criticism of his child, and you're not going to win this argument no matter how hard you try. Let the parent blow off some steam, and then merely thank her for her time.

Unfortunately, the child ultimately suffers, but perhaps you can be more patient with the child the next time he comes to practice. You may even ask him if anything interferes with his enjoyment of practice or the games. Maybe he can tell you what the problem is even though his parents can't.

Recognizing and Handling Typical Excuses

Practice is tomorrow, Saturday morning, at 9 a.m. You're the coach. Your practice session is totally planned, prepared, and ready to execute. You come home from seeing a movie Friday night and note a few new messages on your answering machine:

✔ "Oh, hi, Coach, sorry to get this message to you so late, but we forgot to tell you that we have a previous family engagement tomorrow morning, and as a result, Joey can't make it to practice or the game on Sunday."

✔ "Hi, Coach. Sorry to tell you this, but we're punishing Max this weekend, and he's not allowed to go to practice or play in the game on Sunday."

✔ "Coach, this is Ivan's father. Ivan's not coming to practice tomorrow or the game Sunday. Sorry."

✔ "Coach, it's Sarah Johnson, Mike's mom. I'm a single parent and both my 9-year-old and 11-year-old have games this Sunday at the same time. I have to drive the 9-year-old to an away game, and Mike is going with me, so he won't be at your game. I'm sorry!"

These kinds of phone calls make a coach want to pull his hair out, because this is a discipline problem — not with the kids, but with their parents! It can be frustrating for a coach to have prepared and organized a practice assuming that the entire team of 14 kids are going to be there, only to discover that only 8 actually show up.

Save yourself a lot of grief and anxiety. Remind the parents throughout the season that if they know that a child is not going to be at practice or a game in the weeks to come, it's a great help if they tell you as soon as possible. If you know who's not coming to practice or a game ahead of time, you can plan your practice schedules and, of course, the game lineup. And if a family has two or more kids playing on different teams and the parent(s) needs some help in getting everybody to their games, let mom or dad know that you can help out — as long as you know about these conflicts well in advance.

Certainly, sudden unexpected events come along in all of our lives — a child gets sick overnight or a family emergency of some sort arises — and you understand that such emergencies can't be foreseen. But for those events that can be seen down the road as potential conflicts, a parent can usually tell the coach about the problem well in advance.

Furthermore, to build some responsibility and accountability with the kids, ask them to call you directly rather than letting a parent do it for them. Tell them that as members of the team, it's their obligation to call you if they can't make a practice or game. For some of the younger kids, this task may seem daunting, but by the time a child is 9 or 10, he or she can usually make this call. Besides being polite, this task also teaches the child an important life lesson: Don't delegate responsibility to other people — make the call yourself!

So what do you do when a kid misses a practice or game? It's difficult to lay down the precise law on this issue, but I offer some guidelines for you to keep in mind. The main factor here is playing time; assuming that every kid wants to play as much as possible in a game, that's your currency of worth.

✔ **Weigh the excuse or alibi accordingly and be fair in using your common sense.** For example, if a child tells you several weeks in advance that she is going to a wedding on that Saturday and won't be able to make practice, you really shouldn't shortchange her too much on her playing time (assuming, of course, that she has been to all the other practice sessions). And if a parent calls you early Saturday morning and informs you that her child became ill with a fever overnight, the same thinking applies.

But if a child doesn't make a practice session on Saturday and you received no call ahead of time, you're certainly within your right to ask the child before Sunday's game why he missed practice. If the child has no solid reason, the punishment might be sitting out an extra quarter of the game. You should also explain to the child why he is sitting out that extra quarter: because it isn't fair to the other kids on the team who did come to practice on Saturday when he didn't. They earned more playing time than he did. Plus, you received no telephone call explaining his absence. Again, these are the kinds of lessons — accountability and responsibility — that you want a child to learn from playing youth sports.

✔ **Bear in mind that the child's age is a factor in deciding an appropriate response as well.** You can be much more forgiving of a 5- or 6-year-old who misses a practice than of, say, an 11- or 12-year-old. Always give the child a chance to explain why he or she missed practice. But, unless it's a valid excuse, you need to enforce a sense of discipline. In the long run, doing so makes a big difference in each child's life.

Chapter 9

Coaching during a Game or Meet

*O*kay, coach, today's the big day! You and your team are eagerly looking forward to actually playing in a real game, and as the head coach, you can feel the team's expectations to go out there, do their best, have fun — and maybe even win! This should be a time of great anticipation, excitement, and enjoyment for kids of all ages!

Getting Ready for a Game or Meet

Before a game or meet, you have to think about everything from getting directions to the game to developing your starting lineup. This section shows you how.

Making some key phone calls

Before you can start thinking about coaching strategies, starting lineups, and Xs and Os, the head coach has to first handle some preliminary planning. Just as you take a few minutes to plan your upcoming practice sessions and what drills you're going to cover (see Chapter 8), you have to find time during the week to make sure that all of the details are worked out for the upcoming game.

A few minutes of preparation, including making some phone calls before the game, can save you all sorts of unnecessary worry and anxiety on the weekend, when the game is actually played. Very few experiences are as frustrating for a youth league coach as getting to game day only to discover the following:

✔ You don't have the proper directions for an away game, and your team gets lost en route.

✔ Both teams are on the field, ready to play, but you look around and find that no official or ref has shown up for the game — a situation that you could have avoided by calling the official or ref during the week.

✔ Your team comes ready to play, but the other team doesn't show up. Desperate to know what's going on, you call the opposing team's coach, only to find out that the opposing team didn't have this game on its schedule for today.

What happens when these all-too-common situations occur? The kids on your team who were eagerly looking forward to playing the game go away deeply disappointed, and the kids' disappointment is matched by that of their parents, who also add a bit of anger into the mix (as in, "How come the coach didn't check to make sure he had the right directions to the game?" or "How come the coach didn't check ahead of time with the other team?"). Even worse, you get that sinking feeling in the pit of your stomach that maybe you could have avoided all these problems if only you had done a little pregame preparation.

Coaching a youth league game involves a combination of responsibilities — tasks that ultimately fall on your shoulders because you're the head coach:

✔ Make sure that your team knows what time the game starts and what time you want them there.

✔ Make sure that players and parents know where the field is located.

✔ Make contact with the opposing team's coach a few days beforehand to confirm that he or she is ready to play your team.

✔ Double-check that the refs or officials know that a game is scheduled.

If you make these calls and you get an answering machine, leave your message on the machine (along with your name and phone number) and ask the coach or ref to return your call so you know that he or she got the message. Bear in mind that just leaving a message on an answering machine doesn't guarantee that your message will get through!

A little preparation on Tuesday night saves you from a lot of headaches come game day on the weekend.

Handling inclement weather

As the head coach, you have to be prepared to move quickly in case the weather conditions on game day are such that you may — or may not — play.

In some leagues, the commissioner makes a blanket announcement whether the games within the league are to be played or postponed on game day. If that's the case, all you have to do is find out from the commissioner as soon as possible on game day what his or her decision is. But in many leagues, the decision to play is left up to the individual coaches. If you're in this kind of league, you have to first call the opposing coach to mutually make a mature decision (*mature* meaning that you don't take any unnecessary chances) about whether to play the game. Factors to consider include:

- ✔ **Field, track, slope, or pool conditions:** Are there large puddles? Is it too windy? Is it too cold? Is there too much snow? Is it going to be too hazardous because of the weather conditions to get to the game?

- ✔ **The forecast:** It's not raining or snowing right now, but are severe storms predicted to be in the area just around game time?

After a decision is reached, you must put the word out to team members and parents. Ideally, you can call upon an assistant coach to help split up the names on the roster and make the calls. And while you make your calls, don't forget to call the official, ref, or umpire to tell them what's going on as well.

Sometimes, a coach will try a telephone "chain" in which one person is called and then told to call the next person and so on. However, these phone chains are chancy at best. All it takes is one person who isn't home to not get the message and the entire chain collapses.

Preparing your scoresheet

Perhaps the most important pre-game preparation you have to do is to put together your *scoresheet*. This document enables you to keep track of who played what position and for how long in each game or meet.

The importance of this scoresheet cannot be underestimated — not because it's so vital to the final outcome of the game, but because it's your only line of defense if a parent comes to you complaining about how little playing time Johnny is getting during the games or asking, "How come all the other kids get to play shortstop a lot more than my child does?" Without that scoresheet, you have no defense to these accusations. Merely saying "I try to be as fair as possible when it comes to playing time" just won't cut it with outraged parents. As such, they'll insist that their child get the lion's share of playing time for the rest of the season — usually at the expense of the other kids.

Few leagues provide this kind of document, so you're left to your own creativity to invent one. No matter what the team sport is, all you have to do is list each kid's name on the sheet, and then divide the game into the number of periods, halves, or quarters in that sport. Make a grid so that you can check off in each box where each child has played in the game through all four quarters (see Appendix B for an example).

As the game goes on, keep track of the kids as they change positions, all the time filling out your scoresheet. (In order to avoid major messes on your scoresheet, bring a pencil with an eraser — never a pen.) If this becomes too great a task, ask an assistant coach to handle the scoresheet for you. But regardless of who handles this task, it has to be done accurately and reliably. That responsibility ultimately rests on your shoulders.

Never throw away your scoresheet, because you never know when a parent may approach you and openly claim that her child is getting shortchanged on playing time. That's precisely when you bring out your scoresheets and show her how much time her son has really gotten. After parents see how fairly you've doled out playing time, they'll probably become much more agreeable.

Determining your starting lineup

When putting together your *starting lineup* (the kids who are playing in the game first), bear in mind that you usually have more kids on the *roster* (a listing of all the kids on your team) than can play at the same time. Also, kids want to rotate and play different positions throughout the game. (Some leagues mandate that kids rotate through the lineup; in other leagues, this rule doesn't exist. Be certain to check your league's rules!)

Suppose you have 15 kids on your soccer roster. The rules stipulate that only 11 kids can play at one time. That means four players are sitting out. The tricky part for you as coach is to make sure that no child sits out more than one quarter before everybody else does, and to make sure that each child gets a chance to play at several positions: up front as a forward, some work on defense, some time at mid-field, and maybe a few minutes as the goalkeeper.

In the majority of youth leagues, this policy is clear. As the coach, you have to rotate the players throughout the games so that every child takes a turn sitting out. That's the other purpose of the scoresheet: to keep track of which kids have sat out of the games and to ensure that you're fair about this distribution.

Keeping good players on the field

Suppose you have kids of varying abilities on your team and they all want to win. How do you keep your team rotating through, and at the same time put forth a competitive effort? By the time you've coached your team for a few practice sessions, you will have a decent idea of who your better players are. Ideally, whenever you put your team out to play, you always keep two or three of your better athletes on the field at the same time. While they all rotate through and sit out at various times, if you plan well enough, you never have to face a situation in which all of your better players are sitting out at the same time. In other words, everybody stills play the same amount of time in a game, and everybody plays different positions. But with a little advance planning, you can map it out so that you always have a competitive team on the field during the game.

Announcing the starting lineup to your team

Before you announce the starting lineup for the day, remind the kids of one key component: It doesn't make any difference what the starting lineup is because everybody is going to play in the game today.

This is important because every kid wants to be in the starting lineup. Perhaps even more significant is the fact that all parents want to see their children in the starting lineup. Indeed, no matter how much a parent demurs and says, "That's okay — I understand if my child isn't starting," the reality of human nature is that she will be disappointed.

To reinforce the point that you're not going to play favorites and give certain kids special treatment, during the very first game of the season, be sure to have your own son or daughter sit out the first portion of the game. That's right — by not putting your own child in the starting lineup on opening day, you send a distinct message to the other kids and their parents that you are definitely not "playing favorites" this season. While this may not be very fair to your own child who hopes to be in the starting lineup, explain it to your child this way: "Everybody has to sit out during the course of the season. It just happens that your time to sit has come up first."

Making Last-Minute Pregame Preparations

Regardless of what sport it is, when you're coaching kids between the ages of 8 and 14, you want them at the field from 30 to 40 minutes before game time. With little kids (ages 5 to 7), you may want to stick with 15 minutes. This extra wedge of pregame time allows a fudge factor in case a child (or his parent) is running a little late or gets lost traveling to the game.

Because most communities have limited field space available to accomodate all of the kids who play youth sports, many times you won't be able to get your team on the field to warm up until the preceding game comes to an end. Because of that, take those 15 minutes before game time to gather your team together and find some extra space on the field to warm up a bit. You can also chat with them briefly to make sure that everybody is healthy, remind them of what they worked on during practice that week, and give them some last-minute instructions regarding the weather conditions, the field, or the other team.

Be brief in your pregame comments. Don't worry so much about pep talks with your team. Most kids are already so psyched up to play in the game that they won't pay much attention to any last-minute speeches you may have prepared. If you want, try to just have one slogan or chant that you can remind the kids about: "Remember, Broncos — it's defense! Defense wins games!" or "Hustle! Hustle after each ball!" In effect, a short, strong reminder of what they should be doing works a lot better than your best Knute Rockne speech.

Coaching during a Game

Bear in mind that the real reason kids look forward to their games is that they enjoy participating in the game — and their parents share in that joy. (This is why you have to keep up your scoresheet all the time — see the "Preparing your scoresheet" section, earlier in this chapter.)

Of course, you want the team to win — and the kids on your team want to win, too. But more importantly, they want to *play* in the game. Their parents feel the same way.

You'll never have a parent come up to you and complain that his or her child is playing too much in the game — but you may get lots of parents who'll tell you right to your face that their children are not getting enough playing time. The fun is in the playing!

Give praise, praise, and more praise to the kids

Yelling and shouting during a game is fine, as long as you offer only words of encouragement and praise. Praise is what the kids want to hear, and praise is what drives them to play at even higher levels of competition. When in doubt as to what to say to the kids, always praise them. And if you can't praise them for winning or doing well, simply praise them for making such a great effort.

Conversely, avoid negative comments ("Jake, what the heck are you doing out there?" or "Mary, you're not trying at all!") and sarcasm ("Do you want to lose? Is that it? You want to be losers?") at all costs. Too many coaches think that using sarcasm helps get kids' attention — or maybe even a few chuckles. But the reality is that most youngsters don't understand a sarcastic approach, and they'll interpret your comments as being mean-spirited and nasty. If anything, instead of becoming motivated, they actually become demotivated.

Act in a sportsmanlike manner

This should go without saying, but unfortunately, coaches sometimes snap during games and begin to act like loudmouthed boors: shouting at refs, umpires, or officials; getting into screaming matches with the opposing coach; or using profanity around the kids on the team.

There's absolutely no reason for this kind of behavior! As a coach, you have to remind yourself before each game that the kids on the team look up to you. If they see you stomping and swearing during a game, they naturally assume that such behavior is not only okay, but desirable. If they observe you verbally blistering an official, they assume that it's okay for them to do the same.

Take a moment just before the start of each game to calmly remind yourself to be a good sport and abide by the rules of sportsmanship, no matter what the outcome of the game is. Those few seconds of pregame serenity will go a long way toward helping you keep your cool.

Set an example

Sure, you're supposed to coach to win. All coaches want to win. But at the youth sports level, you should be coaching to win within certain acceptable parameters. That means that you should set an example on the sidelines that gives you (and your team) a solid reputation as someone who not only believes in the rules of the game and in sportsmanlike behavior, but also follows the rules of the game and of sportsmanlike behavior.

That isn't always easy. Many volunteer coaches have a difficult time separating their own emotional desire to be the winning coach from doing what's right on the field. Here are some examples:

- Moments when you know, deep down in your heart, that you ought to be putting a weaker player into the game — but you hesitate to do so because you fear that your team may lose the game.

- Moments when the ref or official makes a wrong call — but the call benefits your team — do you say anything to correct the situation or do you just keep quiet?

- Moments when you're tempted to juggle the game schedule so that your team can benefit from playing a weaker slate of opponents.

When these moments occur during the course of the season — and inevitably they will — you have to ask yourself what is the right thing to do. For some coaches, there's very little debate. Good coaches wonder how their responses to critical situations are going to affect not only them, but also the kids on the team. These coaches ask themselves, "Is winning the fifth grade boys' basketball championship really more important than doing the right thing?"

These are introspective questions that only you can answer. But before you do, go back and ask yourself why you decided to coach the kids in the first place. Was it winning the league championship that motivated you? Or did you volunteer because you thought that it might be fun, not only for the kids but for you as well?

Monitor the opposing coach's behavior

You can't control the other coach — but that doesn't mean that you have to accept bad behavior on the sidelines. During your tenure as a coach, you will probably observe a variety of opposing coaches. Some will scream and yell at their players, some will try to intimidate the officials, and some will even accuse you of not playing by the rules.

In short, because you can't control the opposing coach, don't even try. The only time you should ever interfere or intervene is when you feel strongly that the other coach has overstepped her boundaries in terms of coaching sportsmanship. Such situations include the following:

✔ The coach uses profanity throughout the game.

✔ The coach is intimidating either your players or the official with her loud behavior.

✔ The coach does or says something that is clearly unsportsmanlike. This includes actions or comments directed even at her own team.

But how do you actively complain about an opposing coach's behavior? Here are some tips:

1. **Call time-out and speak to the official or ref.**

2. **Explain your concerns about the opposing coach.**

   Usually, the official will agree with you and will then quietly say something to the opposing coach in order to calm her down.

3. **If this approach doesn't work, try again, only on this second go-round, tell the ref that unless the opposing coach starts behaving in a mature fashion, you're going to be tempted to remove your team from the field.**

   Although this is a strong request, it's also a fair one. There's no reason for a coach to act in a childish, obnoxious way — especially in front of children and their parents. (If your league has adopted a zero-tolerance policy, this is the perfect time for the official or ref to enforce it. See the following section.)

4. **Assuming that the opposing coach finally gets the message, you have every right to report her behavior to the league board of directors.**

   Chances are you won't be the first one to have complained about her sideline antics. It's then up to the league directors to take action to reprimand the coach.

Adopt a zero-tolerance policy for parents

In order to put some real support into making sure that coaches, parents, and fans abide by the rules of good sportsmanship in youth leagues, more and more leagues around the country are beginning to enforce a *zero-tolerance policy*. This policy puts the game fully into the hands of the official, ref, or umpire who's working the game. If a coach or parent becomes unruly on the sidelines and begins verbally abusing the ref, the ref can stop the game at any time and announce to the teams, coaches, and parents:

> "This game will come to an end immediately and be forfeited unless that gentleman in the white shorts in the third row gets up and leaves the field . . . now! You have 15 seconds to leave or this game is over."

As you may imagine, when the ref stops the game and makes this loud announcement, everybody is usually stunned for a few moments — especially the individual who has caused the disruption. But if the ref sticks to her position and doesn't waver, she can simply count off the ticks on her watch until the rowdy individual gets up and leaves. Even if the ref is a teenager who's blowing the whistle on a grown-up, the zero-tolerance rule is most effective.

This policy, which should be made clear to all parents and coaches at the start of the season via a newsletter or flyer that accompanies each child home, has a remarkable effect. It turns the pressure away from the ref — and places it squarely on the disruptive coach or fan. What's more, as soon as the ref threatens to end the game immediately, the fan in question has to decide whether it's worth making a bigger jackass of himself (and becoming the focus of all the other parents' — and kids' — anger for having caused the game to be forfeited) or to just get up and go.

Usually, the fan or coach is so stunned by this sudden turn of events that he decides to get up and leave. Yes, he may add a few choice words on the way out, but he knows now that he's been challenged by the ref and that the ref has done the right thing. (By the way, many times when the ref ejects this unruly fan from the field, the other parents spontaneously break into applause for her actions.)

If this kind of coach, parent, or fan has been bothering your league, talk to the board of directors about instituting this zero-tolerance policy. It has worked quite well where it has been used, and it keeps the unsportsmanlike behavior under control. Zero tolerance may seem like a rather extreme policy to administer in youth sports, but the reality is that, in this day and age, it's probably needed more than ever before.

Handle a child's inappropriate behavior during the game

Sometimes, in the heat of battle, a child momentarily loses control of his emotions. He may be frustrated by an opponent's defense or have difficulty with a ref's call. The child may do any number of things to voice his frustration, including saying something he shouldn't or doing something physically that is strictly off-limits.

When this occurs, many times the ref, ump, or official stops the action and admonishes the child right there. But sometimes the ref doesn't say anything, and as the coach, you feel you should. If this occurs, immediately remove the child from the game and let him cool off a bit. Explain to him why he is getting this "timeout," and let him sit. Invariably, the child will complain openly about this: "It's not fair, Coach, the ref isn't make the right calls" or something along those lines. This is the perfect opportunity to explain to the child (and his teammates):

> "Sometimes, life isn't fair. And the same goes for sports: You have to make up your mind whether you want to keep playing, even though all the calls don't go your way, or whether you just want to sit out on the sidelines and complain about how unfair it all is. Make up your mind — because that's the way it is."

This may be a harsh lesson for kids, but ultimately it's one of those issues that they'll have to grapple with. Part of being a coach is teaching the kids these difficult lessons.

What about the youngster who is taunting or trash-talking her opponents? Again, don't wait for the ref to intervene. Just have the child come sit next to you on the bench, and remind her of how you want her to play the game:

> "But coach, trash-talking doesn't mean anything — it's just part of my game!"

> "Perhaps, it is, Jill, but I'm the coach, and on my team, none of my kids does any trash-talking or taunting. That's just the way it is. If you want to play, you have to play by my rules."

Of course, the child won't like this. But after she sees that you mean business and that the other kids are abiding by your rules, she'll fall right into line.

The Post-Game Wrap-Up

You've done your pregame homework, you've kept your scoresheet, and hopefully your team has played a good game along the way. Now, as the game comes to a close, it's up to you to make sure that all your kids put together a fine show of sportsmanship.

That usually means bringing the kids together in a huddle as the game comes to a close. You want to tell them what a great effort they put forth, how well they performed, and how proud they should be of themselves. This post-game praise should take no more than 20 seconds, but it should be sincere, and you should make eye contact with each of the kids.

Then it's always appropriate to give a "2-4-6-8, who do we appreciate?" kind of team salute or cheer for the other team, regardless of which team won the game. Make it a standard policy that you lead your team over, in a line, to shake hands with the opposing players. After you lead off by congratulating the other team, look back to make sure that your kids are taking this procedure seriously and that no one is being disruptive or discourteous. In other words, make it clear to your team that sportsmanship is an important part of playing sports. If you can, also make it a point of thanking the ref or umpire for doing a good job.

Congratulating some of the parents of the other team also sets a nice tone. Why is this so important? Because the kids are observing your behavior. They take their cues from you. If, especially after a tough loss, they see you — their coach — making a sincere effort to put aside your disappointment to go over and offer congratulations to the other coach and team, they begin to get the idea of what is appropriate behavior after a game.

If, on the other hand, you whine and complain to your team that "We got jerked around today by the ref!" or "The other coach was cheating!" or "Their team definitely had players who shouldn't have been on the roster!" you're telling your kids that it's more appropriate to find reasons and alibis for losing than it is to simply acknowledge, "Today just wasn't our day — it was theirs."

Unfortunately, kids often pick up on your visual and verbal cues during these down moments, and that's where the pressure is really on you (and the other team parents) to say and do the right thing. In the long run, that will be the major part of your legacy as a coach.

Delivering your post-game postmortem

Some coaches want to do more than just have the kids get together and congratulate the other team after a game. Some want to take their team to the side and go over a lengthy postmortem of what they did right and what they did wrong — in short, review the game from beginning to end.

If you're ever tempted to do this, forget it. It doesn't work at the professional level, it doesn't work at the college level, and it certainly doesn't work at the youth level. Kids just don't want to sit around after a game and hear you vent about blown coverages on defense or how they didn't come to win today. Such filibustering may allow you to blow off some steam, but the children will quickly tune you out and start to daydream about what they're going to do the rest of the afternoon. The last thing they're going to think about is the game they just played. (In addition, too many parents want to give their own post-game analyses to their children in the car on the way home. See Chapter 3 on the problem with post-game analyses.)

So, Coach, just let it go. Let the kids be kids! You can make mental notes about what they have to work on at next week's practices, but now's not the time to dissect the game.

Part III
Motivation and the Mental Game

The 5th Wave — By Rich Tennant

HOME VISITOR
2 1 6

"Hey! When I said take out the person who's making us lose, I didn't mean the scorekeeper!"

In this part . . .

Coaches often search for the right words to motivate their youngsters. (The same applies to parents who have athletically gifted kids.) This part provides key motivational insights into how your children actually view an athletic contest and how they see themselves as participants in these sporting events. Along the way, the issue of good sportsmanship and appropriate behavior — for coaches, parents, and the kids — are all explored in detail, with lots of practical suggestions and recommendations.

Chapter 10

Motivating Today's Young Athletes

Motivation is the essence of coaching, and your greatest motivational tool is the language you use with your team. The reason you're trying to communicate effectively with the kids on your team is because you want to motivate them to play their best.

Consider these two motivational approaches to a 12-year-old basketball player. In both cases, it's the same player. But ask yourself this: If you were a 12-year-old, which coach do you think would motivate you to player better? (Hint: If you can't answer this question, ask one of your kids to help you.)

> Coach #1: "Peter, you've been playing great all year for this team, and I just want you to know that it's terrific fun to watch you perform. And with your athletic potential, wow — you have some future ahead of you."

> Coach #2: "Hey, Peter — when in the world are you going to start working hard? Why, you've got all the potential, but the truth is, you just aren't living up to it. And if you ask me, that's a real shame."

You're dealing with children here — not grown-ups! Kids today want to hear praise, praise, and more praise. They just aren't going to respond to harsh criticism or negative motivational techniques — especially if it comes from a coach. You may be absolutely convinced that your giving that "lazy kid" a "little kick in the butt" is the best thing for his motivation, but you have to remind yourself that you're dealing with a child. What works with grown-ups doesn't always work as well with kids.

"Motivating" by Yelling — Why It Doesn't Work

Does the following sound familiar?

"That's it, Sally, now make the pass over to Rebecca now. Pass it! Pass it! Okay, Rebecca, watch it, watch it! You're dribbling too much. Look out for that other player! C'mon, girls, absolutely nobody is hustling out there! Pass it! Pass it! Becky, would you please pass the ball to Michelle!"

This is how too many youth coaches "motivate" their players. This kind of motivation is just loud — and annoying to both players and their parents. Yet, it's also extraordinarily common.

Indeed, one of the striking ironies of coaching kids is that so many coaches assume that the only real way to communicate effectively and motivate a player is to raise their voices and holler at children if they want the kids to pay attention. It happens everywhere. On any given game day all over America, you can find youth coaches screeching at the highest decibels, trying to instruct a young athlete on how to make a play or how to stop an opponent from scoring. In some cases, the noise that the coach makes drowns out all the other sounds of the game: the kids running back and forth, the applause and cheering from the parents, and even the occasional whistle from the ref.

Plenty of youth coaches also believe that if a youngster doesn't adapt to his particularly rigid coaching style or philosophy, then the kid can simply quit. "We don't have time or patience for kids who don't want to work hard and hustle," is the typical response from this kind of hardened coach, "We make it clear that we only want those youngsters who want to play — and play hard all the time." And if a particular kid doesn't shape up or show the kind of motivation that the coach demands, the coach either cuts him from the team or gives him so little quality playing time that the kid ultimately just gives up and quits. (This dogmatic approach occurs more often at the older, travel-team level rather than with kids just starting out in sports, but even by the tender age of 10 or 11, plenty of coaches approach kids in this style.)

Unfortunately, this loud-mouthed approach to coaching kids isn't very effective — it's often more destructive rather than constructive. Kids just don't like being yelled at, and in terms of effective communication, this coaching style is probably a lot more outdated than most coaches would like to admit.

"Nonsense!" some youth coaches say. "The only way to keep these kids under control and in line is to keep a sense of verbal discipline with them. And if I have to raise my voice every so often, well, that's a small price that they'll have to pay."

Perhaps. But you can definitely maintain a strong sense of discipline on your team, and you can do it without being loud.

How the best coaches motivate

Contrast the nonstop verbal coaching style with some of today's most successful professional coaches:

- ✔ Ever see New York Yankees' manager Joe Torre work a game? He sits and watches every inning and all the good plays and not-so-good plays that his team makes without ever changing his expression. There's no yelling, screaming, or posturing: Torres just sits and watches all the action. Sure, he's the first to admit that his insides are churning like pistons, but he never shows his inner angst to his team. Maybe that's why the Yankees and Joe Torre are so successful.

- ✔ Same goes with Phil Jackson, who won six championship rings with the Chicago Bulls. Ever watch Jackson coach a game? He calmly sits, watches, and observes. There's an inner peace within Phil — he realized a long time ago that shouting and yelling at his players not only isn't productive — it's downright counterproductive.

- ✔ Indiana Pacers' head coach Larry Bird never shows any emotion, and he has said many times that he couldn't stand it as a player when coaches raised their voices. UCLA's legendary John Wooden never yelled at his players. Dean Smith of the University of North Carolina wasn't loud. Buck Showalter of the Arizona Diamondbacks is quiet. So is Bobby Cox of the Atlanta Braves. And on and on.

So why don't more coaches use the quiet approach?

Yes, a few highly successful loud coaches are still around — Bobby Knight of Indiana, just to name one notable coach. But these days, the yellers and screamers are becoming more the exception rather than the rule. So the question is this: If so many great and successful coaches are recognized these days as non-screamers, how come so few youth coaches try to imitate that calm style?

Most likely, this harsh motivational technique has its roots in the coach's own athletic background. There was a time during the 1950s and 1960s when the most respected coach in sports was the venerable Vince Lombardi. Lombardi, who was the legendary coach of the Green Bay Packers, has been misquoted for years as having said that "Winning isn't everything . . . it's the only thing!"

Along with that misquote (he actually said "It's the will to win that's everything"), the Lombardi legend has been somewhat embellished over the years. But upon closer inspection of Lombardi's actual coaching technique, while he portrayed himself as a stern and tough taskmaster in front of the entire team, he really got to know each of his players on a highly individualized basis. By knowing them on a one-to-one basis, he was then able to build a rapport and make a connection with them. That gave Lombardi the keys to know how to individually motivate such top former NFL players as Paul Hornung, Bart Starr, Willie Davis, and Jerry Kramer. That was his real motivational strength.

Unfortunately, as the myths have grown surrounding Lombardi, many of the kids growing up in that era simply assumed that the best way to motivate athletes was to scream, yell, deride, and verbally push them in the so-called "Lombardi style" of coaching.

What ever happened to those kids from those long-gone days? Simple. They grew up and they became parents — parents who now patrol the sidelines of youth league sports competitions.

How to Talk to Young Athletes Today

Internet. Sega. Cable television. Satellite dishes. Chat rooms. Sound bites.

Parents and Coaches, face it: Words like these never existed when you were growing up. But they are certainly part of every kid's lifestyle today. As such, as a parent, you have to adapt and speak their language; otherwise, you'll be left behind when trying to communicate with kids today.

Adapting your language also applies to knowing how to talk with kids in the world of sports. It takes a little effort and a little forethought, but work from the premise that your words, voice inflections, and verbal emotions can have a major impact on a child's life — the following sections can help.

Speaking at their level — not down to them

Nobody likes being spoken "down" to. Not even kids. Because you likely tower — quite literally — over the kids on your team, try getting down at their level by bringing all the kids together in a tight circle around you, crouching down on one knee, and then addressing them. This simple maneuver allows you to do several things:

> ✔ **You can make eye contact with each child on their level.** Making eye contact is the best way to start building a sense of trust and motivation with a child. If you find a child who is looking down or off into space, you can keep looking at him until he realizes that you're speaking directly to him — that child will start paying attention.

> ✔ **Because the kids are in a close circle around you, you don't have to raise your voice.** In fact, some coaches actually prefer to speak in such a quiet tone that the kids find themselves leaning forward to hear what the coach is saying. You won't have a problem keeping the kids' undivided attention with this approach — they'll be leaning forward on their tiptoes trying to find out what you're saying.

Try these approaches early in the season. You can, of course, modulate the level of your voice to see how loudly (or softly) you have to talk to keep them riveted. But all children would much prefer to have a calm, almost grown-up conversation with their coach than to have you stomp, yell, and scream at them.

Treating kids with respect

Talk to your team as though they're young men or women. Talk to them with a sense of dignity and maturity, keeping in mind that you're all aiming for the same unifying goal.

Let them know that you're there for them, all season long. Much like a teacher in a classroom, the kids look upon you as one of the few grown-ups in their young lives that they respect and respond to. Instinctively, they'll want to please you — so keep that instinct alive. Show respect for them and they'll begin to have confidence in themselves.

A 9-year-old comes up to you and proudly proclaims, "Coach, I want to play shortstop today. My favorite player is Alex Rodriguez, and I want to see what it's like playing short, okay?"

You look at the 9-year-old, and you know in your heart that he's not the most athletically gifted child on the team. You aren't certain he can even reach first base with a throw, assuming he can even catch a ground ball. As such, you have an immediate decision to make: Do you give the kid a chance to play short, or do you gently tell him "Maybe later in the season, son, but not today."

The right choice? Show some confidence in the kid! Give him a chance to pursue his childhood dream and let him play shortstop. Coach, don't worry so much about whether he can actually play the position well, or whether the team will suffer from his presence in the field. That's really not the purpose of youth sports in the early years. It's supposed to be about kids chasing their own dreams, finding out for themselves just how good (or perhaps not so good) they are, and discovering which aspects of their game needs work and in which aspects they excel.

But it all starts with you giving that kid both the chance and the respect to go out on that field and try.

Remembering that there's no "I" in team

Remind your players that they're on a team, and that it's the team that comes first ("There's no 'I' in 'team'") and that if they — as a team — want to have some success this season, it will only be because the team as an entire unit has played well.

Don't worry if they're just starting out at age 5 or 6, and that you aren't certain that you're getting the message across to them. That's okay. What is important is that they're exposed to this kind of team message early in their sports experiences, so that they become gradually comfortable with it.

Eventually, as they mature, this concept will make more sense to them, as they'll realize that for any team to succeed, there has to be a mutual understanding of trust among players. For example, in the early stages, lots of kids will try to control all the action by themselves. You'll see this happen when a kid hogs the ball: A soccer player takes the ball the length of the field, never looking to pass off, and then shoots on the goal. All of the other kids plea with the child to pass the ball, but the child refuses to do so.

This selfish style of play begins to phase out when kids reach the age of 10 or 11. They begin to understand that they can play more effectively by passing the ball or puck. They also begin to see how coaches, parents, and their teammates appreciate a well-placed pass more than the actual goal or basket itself. That's all part of the process of becoming a mature, accomplished athlete.

As the coach, make a big deal out of the kid who makes that terrific pass or puts the team's glory ahead of her own. Make it your job to salute such fine efforts.

Using good performances to discuss criticisms

Casey Stengel, the great Hall of Fame manager who's best known for his success with the New York Yankees, used to be at his crankiest whenever his Bronx Bombers won a game. When the game was over, Stengel would be tough on his players if they didn't execute some cutoff plays perfectly, missed some signs, or didn't hustle enough. He just wouldn't tolerate any small screw-ups or miscues by the Yankees.

"Casey, why are you so tough on your players?" asked one of the veteran sportwriters who covered the Yanks, "After all, they're winning all the time, and winning championships for you. Why do you criticize them about the way they play?"

Stengel would smile and reply, "Because it's a lot easier to hand out criticism to your players when they're winning than when they're losing."

TIP

Truer words were never spoken. As a coach yourself, keep that advice with you. It's always a lot easier to approach and discuss minor flaws or problems in your team's game when the team is doing well. After a win, the team's spirits are always higher, the kids feel good about their victory, and their overall mood is much more easygoing and open. This, then, is the precise time to go over some of the flaws, mistakes, or miscues from their game — many of which are often overlooked when the victory is sealed. Indeed, more often than not, the winning team's mistakes are simply forgotten by the warm afterglow of having won the game.

EXAMPLE

Here's a sample script as you bring your victorious basketball team together after the game:

"You were exceptional today. You played well, and the final score speaks for itself. I couldn't be happier for you.

"But as we go home and celebrate our win today, let's not forget some of those moments in the game where we still continue to have some problems. For example, we still aren't hustling back fast enough on defense. It didn't hurt us today, but we may get burned later on in the season by a quicker opponent. Please don't forget — get back in a hurry on defense.

"And our ball movement was much improved today. You are all passing the ball better and better. But that being said, we can still move it faster, quicker, and better. I'm looking for those players who know how to see the entire court and can find the open person with the ball. Remember, at some point this year we'll probably play a team that likes to use a full-court press. We have to be ready with our passing skills when that happens.

"So, again, my heartiest congrats on a job well done, but remember that we aren't finished yet. We're getting better all the time — but we just have to keep working."

This kind of approach allows for smiles all around, but it also sets the stage for your next practice. You've already let them know that you aren't going to forget about some of the weaker parts of their game that need to be addressed.

But you let them know — they can still enjoy the moment, yet look ahead to the next game with hopes to do even better.

Helping young athletes when they're disappointed

This is a part of the job that no coach enjoys. What in the world can you say when

- ✔ Your kids have just lost a close, hard-fought game.
- ✔ Your goalie just let in the winning goal, and he's in tears.
- ✔ Your top swimmer just came in a most-disappointing fourth place.
- ✔ Your centerfielder just struck out for the third time in the game.

Failure. Disappointment. Frustration. No matter what you call it, it's an emotion that is very much a part of sports — especially at the youth level. But unlike most professional athletes (most of whom know how to deal with disappointment), kids are tasting these bitter emotions for the first time.

As a caring coach, you have to have a degree of sensitivity of what to say to a young boy or girl who is having a tough time. First, make certain you have your own emotions under control. You're not going to be very effective in communicating with the kids on your team if they see you whining, complaining, or becoming downcast when faced with a downturn in the game. Get yourself in order first.

Think for a few moments on what you want to communicate. Try to gauge just how upset the kids really are before you speak with them. Some kids may get frustrated, but their personality make-up is such that they just get up, dust themselves off, and they hustle back into the action. Other kids, however, will have tears streaming down their cheeks and will give every indication that they want to run off and hide.

When you spot tears, go to the child and try to discreetly move them away from the rest of the team (you don't want any "Hey, what's wrong with Mike? How come he's crying?" coming from the kid's teammates). Then, after he's off to the side, crouch down on one knee so that you can talk quietly with him. Reassure him that frustration and setbacks are just part of the game. Ask him whether he wants to keep on playing. More times than not, he'll nod yes. Give him a moment to compose himself, let his tears dry, and then let him run back into the game.

Here's an example for consoling the 9-year-old goalie who just gave up an easy goal:

> "Samantha, are you okay? Are you hurt? (She shakes her head no, even though she's crying.) Well, let me tell you this: Every goalie who has ever played the game of soccer has given up goals, so there's nothing to be ashamed of. Goals happen in soccer. I think you're doing a terrific job for us as the goalkeeper, and I want you to keep playing there for us. Can you do that for us?"

What's happening here is that you're both giving Samantha a chance to deal with her frustration as well as reassuring her that it's okay for her to stay in and to keep playing. You're also giving her some time to realize that the world has not come to an end. Within a few moments, she'll get back to her position and will most likely redouble her efforts to play well.

After a tough loss or disappointing finish, as the coach, you may be tempted to want to say a lot, but this is not the time to drone on and lecture the kids. Instead, bring the team together in a tight circle. Be brief in your comments, but select your words carefully and put emphasis into them. Emphasize your team's effort that day, how well they played, but also how well the other team played.

Take no more than two minutes, tops, for this post-game chat. If you want, rather than lecture them, ask what they think they did well as a team, and likewise, what they think they did poorly. Give them a chance to talk. Then tell your troops to keep their heads up, get some rest and some food, and look ahead to the next game. Say something like the following:

> "I just want you to know how proud I am today of each and every one of you. Each one of you played hard, hustled for the entire game, and did your job. That's all any coach can ask of you — in fact, it's all you can ask of yourself. But the other team also played well today, and let's give them some credit. Nobody beats you without having a terrific game, and today they had a terrific game. So, take it easy on yourselves. Go home, shower up, get something to eat and drink, and let's put this one behind us. Let's look ahead to our next game, because we'll be ready for that one."

Forget your lecture. The kids have no use for it after a game, especially a game they just lost.

Encouraging a team that's always losing

Yes, it happens. Whereas most youth leagues do their best to ensure that all the teams in the league are well-balanced in terms of talent, sometimes one team just falls through the cracks and finds itself almost always on the short end of the scoreboard.

Perhaps one of the better players on the team gets injured early in the year. Maybe another good player moves with her family out of town. Or perhaps some of the kids on the team were a bit overrated (in terms of their talent) when the league made up the teams. Whatever the reason, the bottom line is that, as the coach, you have to do something to keep the kids enthused and motivated to continue playing.

To accomplish this difficult task, make the games — and especially the practices — as much fun as possible. After all, if the team loses game after game, it won't be long until you'll see some of the players not show up for practice, or even worse, decide not to show up for the games.

Some coaches just turn their back on such a situation — because, quite frankly, they don't want to be there either! But if you want to do the right thing, take a few moments to add some levity and creativity into your team's practices and game. Here are a few suggestions:

- ✔ **Schedule a parents versus kids scrimmage game for one practice session.** This keeps the kids (and their parents) enthusiastic about coming to practice.

- ✔ **Organize a mini-Olympics of sorts for the kids on your team.** Set up one practice where you divide the team into two units, and then let the two teams compete against each other — like a color wars competition. The challenges should be basic drills from the sport they're playing. At the end of practice, you can hand out two packages of gum or two candy bars to the winning team, and one package of gum or candy to the losing side.

- ✔ **Set up a practice session (especially on a rainy day), during which you show a videotape to the team.** You can start the indoor session by showing some instructional videos, but then, just as the kids start to get bored, break out some home videotape of them playing in a game. All you have to do is ask one of the parents to shoot one or two of their games early in the season (and make certain they get every kid on tape), and then edit it a bit to show to the kids.

The purpose of all these creative sessions is to let the kids enjoy themselves and to look forward to going to practice. While this takes a little more effort from you, it can make all the difference in the world to the kids.

EXAMPLE

"It's all in their heads . . . "

Here's a true story: On a very hot, sunny spring day, when the temperature was hovering in the 90s, my 11- and 12-year-old girls soccer team wanted to do anything except play soccer. They said, "Coach Wolff, it's just too hot. We don't want to run up and down a field where there's no shade. Do we have to play today?"

I came up with this different kind of approach: "Girls, remember a few months ago when we played on that very cold and windy day? Most of you were begging for blankets and hot chocolate during the game. Well, let's try that same approach today — just imagine that it's still very, very cold, and that you're freezing out there. In fact, the hotter you get, the more you think and talk about hot drinks, warm jackets, and blankets. Not only will this mental approach get you in the right frame of mind to play, but it'll confuse the girls from the other team — who are just as hot as you are."

The girls laughed, but promised they would try it for a half. And it worked! Not only did this ploy distract the girls from the oppressive heat, they couldn't wait to come over to the sidelines and, in jest, say to their parents, "Oh, I'm so cold out there. Did you remember to bring along a thermos of hot chocolate or tea?" By halftime, the girls were laughing at the lunacy of all this, but they were still playing hard in the hot sun — even as their opponents were wilting.

By the time the game was over, my team was trying to top themselves in search of heat. One girl wanted to go home and take a hot bath right away; another was complaining to her mom about her fingers being frostbitten, and so on. The girls won that day — all thanks to a little creative motivational twist on the weather.

(Of course, as the coach, always keep an eye on the weather — especially if it's extremely hot or cold. Use common sense.)

On game days, break your team's performance down into periods of play. That is, try to get them to see if they can play hard for each quarter. Tell them: "All I want you to do today is to see if you can outplay this other team for this first quarter. If you can do that, or hold them in check, then we'll be doing great. And don't worry about the second quarter — we'll worry about that quarter when we get to it." In other words, think of different ways of how the kids can approach the game. A different game plan, along with loads of coaching enthusiasm, can motivate them to play their best.

Motivating an individual young athlete

Does the following sound familiar?

- ✔ "My daughter is a terrifically talented young tennis player, but she doesn't seem to want to practice her sport."

- ✔ "My 12-year-old boy is a natural at basketball. But I find I have to push him to go out and practice in the backyard."

Are there magical words or formulas that a parent can use or follow to ensure that one's son or daughter develops such a passion or love for a sport that he or she just can't wait to go and practice their craft? Unfortunately, no. It just doesn't happen that way in sports, and for many hopeful parents, this can be a very sobering reality — that their children, although showing signs of talent, just isn't drawn to the sport with the kind of inner fire that will propel them to the highest levels of competition.

Over the years, well-meaning moms and dads everywhere have tried to push their little athletes into practicing their sports. Some try all sorts of psychological gimmicks and techniques; some even offer financial incentives. ("Son, I'll give you $25 for every goal you get this season.") But despite the parental pleas and proddings, the bottom line remains the same: Unless your son or daughter has an internal desire to go out and practice the sport, there's not much you can do as a parent to foster that feeling.

Does this mean you should just stand by and say and do nothing? No, of course not.

- **Expose your child to a variety of physical activities and sports.** After all, your child may not warm up to the idea of becoming a football player, but you may find that he is developing a passion for mountain biking or snowboarding. Great. If he likes doing it, and wants to stay with it, it's your job to allow him to chase his dreams. Sure, it may not be your favorite sport or game, but then again, this isn't about your childhood — it's about your kid's.

- **Let your child know that he appears to have some particular ability for a sport and praise him for his God-given natural talents.** In fact, as a parent, this is part of your job. If he has a special talent, let him know it.

- **As the child gets older, into junior high school and beyond, communicate to him that his natural God-given talent will only take him so far.** Let him know that if he wants to seriously compete in his sport, at some point he's going to have to spend some time practicing to get better and to hone his skills.

  If your child already enjoys being involved in the sport on a regular basis, it shouldn't take much of a parental push to keep him focused. On the other hand, if your teenager is less inclined to go out and work on his sport, this is a definite sign that perhaps his original infatuation with the game is beginning to dwindle.

- **Know when to back off your child!** You have to develop a sense, as a parent, as to when to stop nagging your kid to go out and practice. You probably didn't like it when your parents pestered you when you were growing up. Your child doesn't want to be nagged by you about going out and practicing his or her sport.

This may even call for a one-to-one conversation with your child about his feelings toward the game, his aspirations in the game, and his life-long dreams. If you do have this conversation, let your child do the bulk of the talking — and you stay away from giving him a lecture. But you can remind him of how much talent he has, and how much time he has already devoted to his skills.

Ultimately, the individual athlete determines just how dedicated and devoted he will be to his sport. As a parent and a coach, you have to abide by his wishes — whether you like it or not. No matter how badly you want the youngster to succeed in sports, inevitably it's his decision — not yours.

Chapter 11

Teaching the Basics of Good Sportsmanship

Consider the following stories that you may have seen in recent sports pages of your local newspaper.

✔ Because of a controversial call by an umpire during an American League Championship Series game between the Boston Red Sox and the New York Yankees, fans in Fenway Park showered the playing field with all sorts of debris. By the time the grounds crew cleaned up the mess, the game had been delayed for well over ten minutes.

✔ When Dallas Cowboys' star receiver Michael Irvin lay motionless on the turf at Philadelphia's Veterans Stadium, some hometown Eagles' fans roared their approval that Irvin was seriously injured. Irvin was later removed from the playing field on a stretcher.

✔ During the prestigious Ryder Cup golf competition at Brookline, Massachusetts, rowdy American spectators heckled Colin Montgomery of Great Britain at every hole, in the hope of distracting him from his game.

The common thread in these stories is sportsmanship — or more precisely, the lack thereof.

People (especially parents and coaches) worry about whether the concept of sportsmanship is extinct. Examples like those in the previous bullets make you wonder. After all, the sad truth is that the parameters of bad sportsmanship are being pushed to the limit, and when young athletes watch sports highlights on television, they may be showered with the latest and most outrageous examples of poor sportsmanship. Kids grow up watching electronic highlights of their favorite stars talking trash, humiliating their opponents, making obscene gestures to fans, spitting on refs or umpires, and so forth.

Kids, in their desire to emulate their favorite players, see that this kind of shocking and abhorrent behavior is not only rarely punished, and in many cases is actually glamorized. And so, kids tend to mimic their role models.

Bad sportsmanship has become so commonplace in America today that it rarely makes headlines, and many fans, parents, coaches, and officials expect these outrageous incidents to occur (and then shake their heads in disbelief). Oddly enough, often when an athlete does exhibit a sense of good sportsmanship, that singular act — probably because it's so rare — becomes the focus of the headlines. This chapter helps you share that vision of good sportsmanship with the kids you coach.

Understanding the Potential Impact of the Youth Coach

As the coach of young athletes, you're in a splendid situation to teach the basics of good sportsmanship. No matter what the sport or the age of the children, you're perfectly positioned not only to go over the fundamentals of good sportsmanship, but also to enforce the rules of appropriate behavior. Both parts of this equation take some time (and in some cases, some courage), but good sportsmanship is one of the most important lessons that you can impart to the team.

Start with the assumption that the kids on your team don't know what good sportsmanship is. This may seem a bit odd, but you have to remember that today's kids are exposed to a lot more negative sports behavior than they are to positive sportsmanship. During one of the first practice sessions, explain to the kids that you expect them to behave in the following ways before, after, and during games and practices:

✔ **Have total respect for your teammates, your opponents, and yourself.** This means no trash talking, no taunting, no jeering, and no sarcastic comments. If you can't think of something positive to say to your teammates or opponents, say nothing at all.

Remind the kids that it's certainly okay to want to go out and do one's best to defeat one's opponent, but it's never necessary or desirable to "get in the opponent's face." There's a real distinction there — and if the kids cross over the line, you have to be there to rein them in.

✔ **Never make physical gestures that are designed to embarrass or humiliate an opponent or official.** Celebrating a touchdown is one thing — making the celebration into a public humiliation for the other team is crossing the line of bad sportsmanship. And these days, refs and umpires and officials will quickly move to penalize any team or player who disobeys this fundamental rule — even if you don't.

✔ **The team will line up after each game, regardless of the outcome, and shake the hands of their opponents.** Remind your team that this is a serious moment in the course of the game, that it's absolutely required, and that you won't tolerate any nonsense. Don't let them run off after a game without having them first line up and congratulate the other team. Or if your child is involved in an individual sport, such as track and field, cross country, swimming, gymnastics, golf, or tennis, get her in the habit of seeking out her direct competitors after a match or meet and offering her hand in congratulations. Teach your child that this is a vital part of being a good sport.

If you think your team isn't doing a good job during this post-game session or they're not taking it seriously, spend some time in your practices in which you actually work on this drill. Split your team into two teams, line them up, and make them practice the art of shaking hands.

✔ **Tell your kids that it's wrong to ever curse, swear, or use profanity during the game — and especially when it's directed at an official.** In most youth and amateur leagues, using profanity results in the immediate ejection of a child from a game — and rightfully so. There is simply no place for swearing in youth sports, and as the coach, it's up to you to enforce this rule. As such, let your team members know before the games begin that swearing is unacceptable and is grounds for immediate dismissal.

Don't be surprised if kids don't understand why they can't swear during practices, games, and meets because many kids are surrounded by this sort of language at home! But while household rules against using profanity may be somewhat lax, I can assure you that the refs and umpires haven't relaxed their standards against it at all: Swearing continues to be solid grounds for instant ejection from the game.

Determining What Constitutes Good Sportsmanship

So what should the kids do to make themselves into good sports? In general, the "golden rule" applies to the application of sportsmanship: Treat others in the same manner that you would like to be treated. This simple rule should be repeated to the kids on your team before every practice and game.

Take the time to point out these positive actions to them as well:

✔ **When an opposing player is injured, show respect to that player by immediately stopping where you are on the field and giving him or her as much time as needed to feel better again.** Point out to the kids that they would want the same courtesy shown to them if they were the injured player.

✔ **It's always a classy move to give an injured player a round of applause if he or she has to be removed from the game.** If it were you, you'd appreciate the gesture as well. If the injury is due to a collision with one of your players, it's essential that your player go over and check on the status of the injured player. That's just common courtesy — courtesy that's expected on the playing field.

✔ **It's okay to chat with officials so long as you treat them with respect and dignity.** Kids sometimes are under the impression that the ref is someone to be despised or hated. That's ridiculous! Tell your team to show them respect, and that they can talk with the ref anytime during a timeout.

✔ **Let your kids know that it's okay to feel bad after a tough loss, but that in spite of their emotional state, they should find the inner courage to step up and congratulate the other team.** Sure, it's painful to watch the other team have its big moment in the sun, but the essence of sportsmanship is being a good sport even when you lose.

Let the kids also know that it's a welcome gesture to salute an opposing player's ability. This tradition is most common today in tennis matches and in golf, where opponents often compliment a fine play by one of their competitors. As the coach, you can even set the pace with your team by complimenting individual players from the opposing team. After your kids start to see this kind of sportsmanship, they'll begin to pick up on your example.

✔ **When the game is over, it's a nice gesture for your team to not only congratulate the other team (win or lose) but also to thank the official.** It's an even more gracious gesture when your team thanks the ref after they've just lost a game! That's the mark of real sportsmanship.

Good sportsmanship begins with you

Don't expect your team to behave well if you're using profanity, screaming at the ref, or throwing a tantrum at the opposing coach. Just as kids copy their sports heroes on television, they're going to copy you and your actions as well. "Don't do what I do on the field: Just do what I say, not what I do" seems to be the credo of a lot of youth sports coaches who think that, somehow, kids will follow these simple instructions, but of course they don't. Actions still speaker louder than words, especially on the playing field.

Before you can start teaching and enforcing the basics of good sportsmanship, you have to first understand yourself that good sportsmanship starts with you. There's no use in trying to preach and teach solid rules of good behavior if you aren't going to follow those rules yourself.

If you find that you have difficulty keeping yourself under control on the sidelines or you aren't certain of how your behavior looks, ask your spouse or one of your assistant coaches to keep an eye on you during the games and monitor your behavior. Instruct them to immediately come over to you if they think you're losing your perspective. Or, to get a real sense of how you act on the sidelines, ask one of your friends or one of the parents to videotape some of the games, occasionally videotaping your behavior during the game. You may think that you're acting like a class coach during the action, but the videotape may open your eyes to an entirely different perception.

. . . and teach the parents well, too

When it comes to sportsmanship, it's hard enough to keep the kids and yourself under control. Keeping an eye on the parents is the ultimate challenge. But the chances of your trying to teach another adult who's in his 30s or 40s how to be a good sport isn't very likely. Of course it's a shame that so many grown-ups just don't understand good sportsmanship, but sadly that's the reality of today's youth sports scene.

What you can do is this: Before the start of each season, when you have that very important first team meeting with the parents (see Chapter 7), make certain that you go over how you, as the coach, expect the parents to behave at each game. In some leagues, where zero tolerance rules are in effect (see Chapter 10), it's important to let the parents know that non-sportsmanlike behavior may actually affect the kids' game — and affect it in a very negative way.

It's one thing if a kid loses control for a second or two. That's almost understandable because, after all, she's a kid. But when a parent loses sight of good sportsmanship, he or she has no excuse. It just isn't acceptable in any form.

Enforcing Good Sportsmanship with the Kids

So what do you do if one of your players engages in trash talking or openly taunts an opponent?

As the coach, the burden to do something falls squarely on your shoulders. After all, if you say nothing to the player, you have tacitly supported his or her actions. Of course, you could take the position that "Hey, it's not my place to reprimand somebody else's kid — that's their job as parents, not mine." But such an attitude is merely allowing the child (and his or her teammates) to assume that such behavior is acceptable.

Don't fall into this role. Instead, step up and do the right thing. If the child's behavior is out of line, let her know. Here's how:

1. **Remove her from the game.**

2. **Ask her if she understands why you took her out.**

   If she knows, let her explain to you that what she did was wrong, and have her tell you — eye-to-eye — why she won't do it again.

   Sometimes, the miscreant child has no idea why you removed her from the game. Be patient and explain what she did and why it was wrong. Let her know in no uncertain terms that such behavior is inappropriate. In other words, take the time to explain the rules of sportsmanship.

3. **Sit her out for awhile so that the lesson seeps in.**

Teaching sportsmanship can involve various methods to get the point across. But no matter what approach you use, the important point is that the youngster fully understands what she did was unacceptable. It's important that the lesson stay with them, so that she doesn't repeat it in the future.

Part IV
Coaching Challenges

The 5th Wave   By Rich Tennant

"Let's see - I'll need some children's aspirin for my players and some sedatives for their parents."

In this part . . .

This part gives you specific solutions on how to handle the most common predicaments that pop up in youth sports. Whether you're coaching your own child, coping with athletic injuries, or handling potentially explosive situations on your team, this part offers some experienced advice — you can even find advice on how to handle your own coaching anxieties, as well as information on how being the coach can affect your role as a spouse, parent, and even a member of the community.

Chapter 12

Handling Tough Situations with Your Team

In This Chapter

▶ Dealing with difficult parents

▶ Coping with difficult kids

▶ Encouraging losing teams

"*H*ow could any of these cute little kids ever cause me a problem? And their parents all seem very nice, too!"

While turmoil may not seem possible at the beginning of the season, a youth coach only rarely goes through the season without at least one parent wanting to "chat" with you about their child.

Which age bracket you coach doesn't have any impact on this phenomenon. Parents can start questioning you about kids as young as 5 or 6 — and they can certainly make you sweat a bit when their kids are 11 or 12. While coaching kids is usually the fun part of the job, dealing with the moms and dads can be quite exasperating.

Understanding the Classic Types of Parents

Experienced youth coaches say that most parents fall into certain categories, covered in the following sections. As a coach, you may want to review these categories so that you can better anticipate what to expect when you get that call at home or you hear a parent ask, "Say, Coach, can I talk to you for a moment?"

The flatterer

These are the moms or dads who figure that the best way to ensure that their child will get "favorite preferential treatment" this coming season is if they — the parents — work hard to become your best friend.

This parent is the first to come over on the practice field, introduce himself to you, tell you how thrilled he is that his child is playing for you, and that "everybody knows you're a great coach." While such words of praise are always welcome, you may become a bit suspicious when this parent always finds himself standing next to you at practice sessions or even at games.

The flattery continues: "Coach, you really are something special with these kids" or "I can't tell you how lucky my son is to have you as his coach" or "How are you able to keep these kids so motivated?"

You get the idea. Before too long, the parent is also telling you — in so many words — that their child is also "clearly one of the better players on the team" or that "my son is a terrific goal scorer" or "How can I make sure he gets on the All-Star team?" After all, the parent figures that because you and he are now "best friends," you recognize how good a player his son is, and that, in the best interest of the team, his son should play his favorite position, be the team leader, and on and on.

As the coach, be gracious with these kinds of flattering parents. Acknowledge their well-wishes and feelings of parental pride for their kids — you can even agree with them that their son or daughter is a talented athlete. But you can — and should — always balance the conversation by adding some words like "We're fortunate to have so many gifted athletes on this team" or "I've got my work cut out for me this season, making sure that all these talented kids get a chance to play the various positions they like."

Make it clear that while you recognize that a flatterer's child is a fine player, you alone are responsible for all the kids on the team. You can do this in a polite, caring fashion. And eventually, the parent will get the point.

The know-it-all

This is the parent who is the self-appointed "expert" on the sport you're coaching. You don't have to wait for her to come over and offer you insights into the game's strategy. She'll be right there, from the very first game to the very last, watching and, many times, speaking right up.

A know-it-all parent will likely tell you how good she was back when she was a kid, how she starred in high school and maybe even in college. She may throw around technical terms in front of you, to see if you know anything about the sport. Even worse, if she detects that you don't share enough enthusiasm for her expert advice and counsel, she may be the first one to criticize your coaching work with the other parents on the sidelines.

What to do with a know-it-all? As with most parents, give her a good five or ten minutes of your time to let her make the point. Don't interrupt her — let her talk. No, you don't have to agree with her, but just listen. Then, after an appropriate amount of time, give her a smile, excuse yourself ("I'm sorry, but I have an appointment I have to get to"), and then take off. This pattern may repeat itself a few times during the season, but as long as you listen with attention to her views and give her a smile, you'll make her feel that she has made her point.

Whatever you do, don't get into an argument with a know-it-all parent. That's counterproductive for everyone involved, and can only lead to bruised egos. Listen with a smile, thank her for her thoughts, and then move on.

The dingbat

This is the misguided parent who thinks he knows the inside strategies of the sport, is particularly gifted in evaluating athletic talent, or can offer invaluable help to make you a much more effective coach. Problem is, he doesn't know the sport or the inside strategies at all!

Here are a few examples:

- ✔ "Coach, we all know that you have to be strong to play football, so I've had my boy lift weights all summer at the local gym. Yeah, I know he's only 9, but I figure the sooner he starts, the better off he'll be. And the way I see it, I think our entire team could benefit from a serious weight-training program."

- ✔ "You know what I'd do with this girls' soccer team if I were you, Coach? I'd make them all run three miles in this 100 degree heat — that'll get them in tip-top shape!"

- ✔ "Coach, I took the liberty of drawing up a starting line-up for you, and as you'll see, the batting order I propose will make your team a lot more competitive in this league."

Dingbat parents can be quite persistent in making certain you acknowledge their presence and their alleged expertise. As the coach, you have to handle such situations quite carefully, because while you don't want to insult anyone, you also want to have the freedom to run the team in an appropriate manner.

Your best approach? Take the dingbat parent off to the side after a practice, and with a nice smile on your face, explain to the parent that while you certainly enjoy hearing his thoughts on game strategies, player evaluation, and the like, the truth is that you volunteered to be the head coach of this team so you can make your own decisions. That kind of coaching freedom is what you enjoy the most about the job, and while you're certainly respectful of the parent's thoughts and suggestions, you prefer to coach the team in the style that you're accustomed to.

While such an approach is never guaranteed to stop the dingbat expert in his tracks, it certainly gives him some pause to reconsider his approach to you. That's why it's a good idea to nip this in the bud relatively early in the season. Otherwise, you may be exposed to his thoughts, comments, and suggestions for the entire year.

The loud-mouth

What do you do, as the coach, when one of the moms or dads becomes excessively loud and obnoxious during the course of a game?

Maybe the parent is taking exception to a ref's call, and she feels that it's her right and obligation to let the ref know he made a terrible call. Or maybe it's a parent who thinks that the other team is cheating, and she keeps up a lively chatter with the other parents on the sideline. She keeps claiming that "Our team is getting robbed out there!"

Whatever the situation, it's apparent that the grownup is out of hand and should be asked to calm down. Question is, if the ref or ump doesn't say anything, who should? More times than not, it falls upon you, the coach, to have to go over to the parent in question and ask her to calm down:

> You: "Ms. Brown, it's not that we don't appreciate your verbal support here on the sidelines, but it's becoming apparent that the ref is getting annoyed."

> Loud parent: "Ah, c'mon Coach, the ref stinks! He's cheating our kids out there, making all those calls against us. I don't care if he's getting annoyed — he's annoying me!"

> You (in a firm voice): "Yes, and nobody shares your frustration more than I do, but believe me, if you don't bring it under control, he's going to stop the game and penalize us because of your behavior — and that really won't be fair to anyone, especially the kids."

Usually, at this point, the parent sees your point of view and pipes down. If the parent doesn't want to abide by your wishes, however, you can discreetly talk to the ref during a time-out and explain to the ref that you've already tried to calm the parent down and that she's just out of control. As such, you can then quietly tell the ref that if the parent is bothering him, he certainly should exercise his right to dismiss the parent from the sidelines. A radical move? Perhaps. But sometimes, it's the only kind of move that will get that loud-mouthed parent's attention.

The comparer

This terms applies to those moms and dads who like to engage you in a conversation about their child, but then immediately want to "compare" their child's abilities and progress with the other kids on the team.

Here's a typical comment, followed by a more subtle approach, from this type of parent:

> "Hey, coach, just between you and me, how do you think my kid is doing? I mean, how does she compare with, say, Sarah or Lisa? I mean, Sarah and Lisa are pretty good players — do you think my daughter is as good as they are?"

> "Coach, it's pretty clear that my boy is doing fine and he's certainly enjoying himself on the team, but I was wondering — don't you think he'd be even more effective if he were on the same scoring line with Billy and Andy? Like I said, my boy is doing fine, but the current kids on his line just don't seem to keep up with him. As such, it just seems to me that if he were teamed up with Billy and Andy, the entire team would benefit."

The parent is looking to you for direct corroboration that their son or daughter is not only a good player, but also one of the better (or even the best) athletes on the team. The parent is keenly aware that because you're the coach (and the one who's presumably going to have a major say regarding All-Star teams or the selection of the team captains and the like), the parent is eager to know precisely how you rank his child against the other kids on the squad.

How do you respond to these inquisitive parents? By simply acknowledging that "Yes, indeed, Mr. Brown, your son is one terrific player — he really works hard for us, and he's only going to get better in the years to come." That's a fine and sincere compliment to give to any parent, and the beauty of it is that you haven't compared his child to any other kid on the team. In fact, you've confirmed that his son is a talented athlete and that he's a dedicated player and that, yes, he'll get better as he gets older.

For the most part, that comment will more than satisfy any parent. But if he presses you about comparing his child with some other child on the team, that's where you want to be careful in what you say. When you start openly comparing kids in a conversation with a parent, it won't be long before your words will come back to haunt you and the other kids on the team. And there's nothing more devastating to a team's morale if the word gets around that the coach is saying certain things about certain players.

Professionally, teachers are never supposed to talk about one student's progress with the parents of another kid. That's just not fair to anybody. The same philosophy applies to sports as well. There really is no good reason for you to share your thoughts about other kids with an individual parent. So, rather than risk it, just don't do it. Besides, all the kids and parents can see for themselves how the kids are doing. You don't need to offer your opinion.

Recognizing the Classic Types of Challenging Kids

Just like parents, you're going to run into certain kinds of children on your team who fall into certain personality types. The following sections give you a quick primer on the more difficult young athletes.

Bear in mind that the vast majority of the kids who play youth sports are an absolute dream to coach: They're enthusiastic, cooperative, and responsive to your instructions; they're punctual; and in general, they're always there to have fun. But a few children on your team may cause you some difficulty. The irony is that you'll probably end up spending more of your coaching time with these "problem players" than you will with the other kids who are easy to coach.

The whiner

Does the following sound familiar?

- ✔ "Oh, Coach, do we really have to run these laps? I really don't feel very well today."

- ✔ "Coach, why do we have to practice so early on Saturday mornings? I like to sleep late and watch TV on Saturday."

- ✔ "How come I have to play the outfield today? I'm a better pitcher than that kid."

Also known as a complainer, the whiner is the child who tells everyone on the team that he really isn't enjoying the experience, and that somehow, you are fully responsible for his having a bad time. As you may imagine, this kind of kid can be very difficult to tolerate; even worse, his negative attitude can influence the rest of the kids.

At the first signs of this kind of behavior, take the child off to the side and ask him — in a firm, but gentle way — if he really wants to be on the team. After he says "yes," explain to him that, as the coach, you're not going to tolerate any complaining or whining, and if that is going to be a problem, perhaps he ought to reconsider whether he wants to be on the squad.

If, on the off chance that he says "no," rather than giving him a stern lecture, ask him again if he really doesn't want to play. Try to find out why he isn't enjoying the season. Then take a moment to call the child's parents to let them know what's going on and find out how they want you to handle the situation. Be gentle in your approach. Nobody wants to see a child quit playing on a team.

With kids who demonstrate this negative behavior pattern, you have to make it clear to them right at the start of the season that you're not going to tolerate this kind of attitude.

If the problem continues, your next stop is with the child's parents. Being diplomatic, gently inquire as to whether the child is enjoying him or herself. The mom or dad may be able to articulate any problems or concerns. If they're unaware of any problems, let the parents know that you have a real concern in motivating the child in practice and in games. Find ways to share the burden of approaching the child so that it isn't just your problem — it's their problem, too.

The egocentric superstar

Chances are, in this day and age of electronic sports highlights, you're going to come across the self-proclaimed egocentric superstar. This is the child who shows tremendous athletic ability for her age bracket, and even more so, she is clearly aware that she's a star amongst her peers.

Sometimes, the child is physically larger and, hence, stronger than her friends. Occasionally, she's quicker or faster. Or maybe her overall athletic coordination is more developed at an earlier age. Whatever the reason, the child has quickly responded to being a top athlete, and enjoys the recognition from being noted as such. So far, so good.

The problems begin when the star athlete starts to take on an attitude that she is above everybody else on the team — that she knows best how to exercise, who should play where, and how to coach the team. Even worse, she may take it upon herself to castigate those kids on the team who aren't playing up to the expectations that the star has for them. This star may also throw a tantrum if she doesn't perform well or if she feels that the official has done her an injustice.

Here's your dilemma: If you don't say anything at all — that is, if you allow the star athlete to go her own way — you're doing the child and her teammates a major disservice. Dealing with egocentric players is a dilemma that all coaches at all levels of sports face these days. But it's only the coaches who don't confront it who end up allowing the problem to fester and grow out of control.

To make certain this doesn't happen to your team, help your team understand fully that discipline is a team concept. Discipline involves playing sports the right way: Nobody talks when you're talking, nobody puts down anybody else on the team, nobody plays merely for their own glory at the expense of the team's. Make this clear to your young athletes and if necessary, repeat it again and again to make certain they get the message.

Have the guts to enforce these rules. If you see your superstar athlete behaving in an inappropriate manner, let her know why her actions are wrong. That's important, because it may never have been explained to her before. If the wrongful behavior continues, have the courage to have the child sit on the bench or take a time-out from practice.

If somebody doesn't instill a sense of appropriate team play in the child early on, the child may never learn it. Over the years, too many youth coaches have looked the other way when a star player has bullied teammates or strutted inappropriately on the field. The coach rationalizes that the child will either act more appropriately as she matures or that the kid's parents will eventually clamp down. But parents rarely clamp down on their kids. In their eyes, all they see is a gifted athlete — one that the coach should be grateful to have on his team. And as far as the child maturing or growing out of this phase, the truth is that this sort of behavior generally becomes worse with age.

The non-talker

Nearly every team has one child who is perpetually shy. He just doesn't say a word. He does as he's told, and he seems to be doing okay, but because he rarely says a word to you, you just can't tell what he's thinking, if he's having fun, or if he's bored.

A non-talker can be quite a challenge: As the coach, you want to build a sense of rapport and trust with him, but if he never says anything to you, never makes eye contact with you, or never shows any emotion such as laughter or a smile, you'll have a hard time connecting with him.

Keep your eye on the non-talker, making sure he's doing okay — that he's at least chatting occasionally with his friends on the team. If he's having some difficulty making friends, try to pair him up with another one of the kids on the team. Do some drills in which the two of them have to work together to complete an exercise. When working toward a common goal, kids invariably start to chat with each other.

In addition, take some time in each practice and game to say hello to the non-talker by name, give him a pat on the back, and praise him. Make him feel that he's a vital and essential part of the team. All kids — even shy ones — like to hear praise about themselves.

To help reinforce that feeling, whenever you lead the team in practice, ask different kids to lead the troops with you. Along the way, make certain you occasionally ask the non-talker to be one of the leaders. By thrusting him into a leadership role, you find out quickly whether you're connecting with him. Most of the time, you'll discover that you are.

The short-attention-span athlete

Sometimes, you coach a child who doesn't pay attention to your instructions. This is the child who is always interrupting the team meeting, who likes to go off by himself during practice, or who tends to tease or interfere with the other kids who are trying to pay attention. While some children may suffer from attention deficit disorder (ADD), which makes paying attention to a teacher or a coach a real challenge, other kids don't suffer from this illness but like to make a spectacle of themselves, turning the spotlight away from the practice drills and onto themselves.

One disruptive child can turn an efficient practice session into a real struggle. Nobody likes having to constantly reprimand a youngster during a practice for not paying attention, but if you find that repeated time-outs don't have any real impact on the child, consider having a sit-down discussion with the child's parents. Explain to the parents that while you enjoy having their child on your team, you could really use some of their guidance to help ensure that these interruptions can be brought under control, or at least minimized. Point out to the parents that you've already tried conventional methods of discipline with little success, and you don't want to jeopardize the relationship you have with their child.

What about pep talks?

Pre-game pep talks — which should take place 10 to 15 minutes before the start of the game or meet — are fine, but most youth coaches make the mistake of droning on and on, long after the kids have stopped paying attention. Instead, keep some of these guidelines in mind:

✔ **Do some planning first.** Pep talks have to be fairly well planned in order to gain maximum impact. Jot down the major points you want to make, and then go back and edit them as tightly as you can. Make your points and move on!

✔ **Be brief.** Pep talks to little kids should be no more than three minutes in length. The shorter, the better.

✔ **Get to the point.** Give your theory as to why the team isn't having much success. Ideally, you can convince them that if the flaw is corrected, they'll have a much better chance of winning.

✔ **Be non-accusatory.** Always avoid pinpointing players by name who haven't performed well. By the same token, don't praise individual players, either. Treat your players like a true team — a team that has to pull together in the same way.

✔ **Be inspiring.** Any pep talk should offer the promise that if the kids continue to work hard, success will happen. End on that promise.

What you don't want to do with a pep talk is lecture the kids, point out the past mistakes that the individual kids on your team made, or talk about your sports experiences when you were a kid. Stick to the point and keep it short.

Usually, the parents are able to offer a solution or two to your dilemma. But even if they are as baffled as you are about what to do about their child, at least they know that you've made a serious attempt to do the right thing. If that's the case, then more discipline and more time-outs are very much in order. Remember — the child is not only disturbing you, he's also disturbing the rest of the kids on the team. And that's not fair to them.

Dealing with A Moody Team

In many youth league organizations, you're often just assigned to a team. As a result, you don't have much to say about the make-up of your team. Sometimes the only child you know you'll be coaching is your own son or daughter (most leagues allow volunteer coaches to coach their own children on the team).

Because you won't know who'll be on your team until the roster is handed out (see Appendix B for a sample roster), it's pretty much just a grab-bag of whether your team's personality is enthusiastic, lackluster, easily intimidated, or out-of-control. If your team is full of terrific, enthusiastic, ready-to-be-coached kids, you're all set. But you may wind up with a challenging team: one that's upbeat today and down in the dumps tomorrow, moody, tough to moti-vate, too laid back, too timid, or just not paying much attention.

What this kind of team needs is a quick injection of enthusiasm. And because you're the coach, you're the one who has to provide it. Here's how:

✔ **Be outwardly enthusiastic and upbeat yourself.** Enthusiasm is conta-gious. When you have the kids do calisthenics and exercise drills to start each practice, make sure you and the assistant coaches join in as well. Have the assistants run laps with you and the children. Show the kids that you're having fun. That's half the battle. If they see you and the other coaches having fun, they'll want to have fun, too.

✔ **Break up some of the drills in practice by splitting the team in two.** For example, instead of just having the kids run sprints to stay in shape, make it into a spirited relay race between two half squads. Get one assis-tant coach to oversee one team, and you run the other half squad. Kids will pep up right away once they're competing against their friends.

✔ **Talk to the parents.** Get them to show some enthusiasm by having them design a team banner that they can bring to each game, develop a spe-cial kind of cheer for the team, or bring along a team mascot.

If the kids want, they can even change their team nickname. Have a team meeting to discuss the matter, and see what the kids come up with. Remember, enthusiasm is the key!

Be sure to enlist the aid of your assistant coach(es). Put them to work, giving them specific assignments to work with individual kids.

Chapter 13

Coping with Kids' Sports Injuries

In This Chapter

▶ Diagnosing on-the-field injuries

▶ Putting together a first aid kit

▶ Helping kids with medical conditions

*W*hen kids play sports, they run the risk of getting injured. Thank goodness that most injuries are relatively minor: a skinned knee here or a bump there. But as the coach, you have some responsibilities when little ones get hurt playing sports.

Above all else, each child's health is your number-one priority. That's your overall rule, and it supercedes everything else on your coaching agenda. Make this priority known to the parents and repeat it as often as you have to so that all the kids and their moms and dads understand where you're coming from.

The Basics: What You Need to Know

When young kids get hurt, they tend to experience a combination of two sensations: pain and fear. For many of the little ones, they have never experienced getting hurt when playing sports before and the process can be a little frightening, even if it's only a banged knee or a scuffed elbow. As the coach, you have to calm and reassure the child as best you can.

You may be able to diagnose the medical ailment rather quickly. Perhaps the child had a soccer ball hit her in the stomach and she had the "air knocked out of her." That can be a scary couple of moments for any child, but your reassuring presence can help soothe her to catch her breath. Maybe a young infielder got a bad hop of a baseball off his shin. Again, you should be there immediately to offer aid and assistance to your player, and with bumps and bruises, have an icepack ready to go (see the "Checking the first-aid kit" section, later in this chapter).

Most of the injuries you'll see will include scrapes, stubbed toes, skinned elbows and knees, an assortment of bumps and bruises, and perhaps an unexpected collision between two players. Fortunately, the vast majority of the injuries in the youth leagues are so inconsequential that the child rebounds quickly — even if just a few moments before she was screaming at the top of her lungs in agony.

Gauging your reaction

What's your first reaction when one of your players is injured during a game or meet? Do you immediately run out onto the field, court, track, or rink to offer aid? Do you wait for a stoppage in play? Do you wait to see if the child gets back on her feet and keeps playing on?

A difficult decision, to be sure, and you have to make your decision almost instantaneously. In general, however, here's my rule: If you have any question in your mind whether the child is injured — slightly or otherwise — don't wait for a stoppage in play. While you really don't want to have a stampede of parents and spectators out on the field, you can hustle out there, see how injured the child is, and then offer some assistance. Especially with younger children (kids 10 and under), the quicker you can get out on the field, the better.

Bear in mind that in some leagues, officials frown on coaches running out on the field to check on a player's health. They insist that the play continue until there's a natural stop in play or until the official blows his whistle so that the player can then be attended to. While I understand and sympathize with the ref's feelings on such matters, I must admit that, with all due respect, I feel that the child's immediate injury is a lot more important and pressing than which team wins the game.

Many times, parents of the downed player will rush out onto the field to attend to their youngster. That's okay, if they choose to do that. Some parents will prefer to stand on the sidelines and wait for your diagnosis. The bottom line is that whatever the parents choose to do should be fine with you. After all, they are the child's parents, and they should determine whether their child needs medical attention. Be careful not to overstep your boundaries as the coach.

Checking the first-aid kit

Oddly enough, you may be surprised to find that your team's first-aid kit is poorly stocked — assuming that your team even *has* a first aid kit. Many leagues don't even provide such vital kits to their teams, either because they forget to have one on hand or because they don't want to add to the league's expense.

If you're the head coach, no matter what age level kids you're coaching, make it a top priority to have a first aid kit, and make certain that it's always stocked each week. Include basic necessities such as ice bags (especially the kind for which you break a seal within the bag and they quickly become cold), several pairs of latex gloves, tape, bandages, anti-bacterial disinfectant, hydrogen peroxide (to clean scrape wounds), eye wash, an Ace bandage or foam wrap, tweezers (for splinters), and a pair of scissors.

In addition, make provisions to have a bag of fresh ice on hand, because the immediate treatment of so many injuries involves having ice available right away. Most of the ice bags that you break the seal to open lose their coldness rather quickly.

Keeping a cell phone on hand

You may, on occasion, encounter an injury that's serious enough to warrant calling an ambulance or emergency medical technician. This is when having a cell phone at the competition or practice is of vital importance. Fortunately, as cell phones become more and more popular, at least one or two people in attendance will have a cell phone available in case of an emergency. As the coach, make certain that either you, one of your assistant coaches, or one of the team parents brings a cell phone to every game — and make sure that it's charged and ready to use. Keep the phone number handy (if you dial something other than 911) in which to call an ambulance or emergency help.

In most leagues, the parents are asked to fill out registration cards of emergency phone numbers (pediatrician, relatives, and so on) just for these kinds of situations — especially if the child's parents don't happen to be at a game or practice. As the coach, you must carry the team's registration cards with emergency phone numbers *at all times* — to games and practices. They won't do you much good if they are stashed at home when you need them on the field.

Responding when kids want to return to action too quickly

Sometimes, despite being injured, kids insist on returning to the action. This can be difficult for you to handle, because the child (often older than 10) is telling you that even though she's injured, she desperately wants to keep on playing. This can place you in a most awkward situation. For example, suppose the child has a bump on her forehead but the youngster is also telling you that she's fine and wants to go back into the game. What should you do?

But I don't want to go back in!

Sometimes, young athletes can develop a real concern about whether they are hurt and whether they should keep on playing in a game. Even if the child appears to be perfectly fine, the child may be reluctant to go back and rejoin the others. This perplexing situation usually occurs with children between the ages of 5 to 9.

For many kids, getting hurt in a game — even if only momentarily — can become the source of a tremendous fear. The good news is that this psychological fear is usually only temporary, and the child often gradually wants to return to action after he has had a chance to reassure himself that he's okay. After he's on the sidelines, he can observe how much fun his friends are having out on the field.

Rule number one: When in doubt, the child sits out. No youth sports game or competition is important enough to risk a child's health. Yes, that may mean that your superstar has to sit out the championship game because of an injury, but are you willing to risk that child's long-term health and sports career just so your team can win a 6th-grade championship? That's a gamble that you don't want to take — ever.

Ideally, if the child's parents are at the game, get them over to the child right away and get their opinion as to what they want the child to do. Whenever you have a question about a child's health, trust *your* instincts, not the child's. Unless you get permission directly from the child's parents to let her go back into the game, follow your own common sense.

Don't be surprised if some parents don't always agree with you. Sometimes, parents on the sidelines — *not* the parents of the injured child — won't share your philosophy and will flat out disagree with you. Their attitude will be, "Oh, c'mon, she's a kid — what's the chance of her getting hurt again? Or getting hurt badly? Besides, we need her back in the game."

What to do? Don't be cowed by the others. Stand firm with your convictions. The only parents you should pay any attention to are the mom and dad of the injured athlete. If they aren't certain about whether their child can play in the game, let them know that you'd feel a lot more comfortable as the coach if they first get clearance for their child to play from their family physician. No, you really can't demand that they have a doctor's note (unless the league has a provision for that), but you can suggest it. This is especially a good idea if the child is coming off an ankle or leg injury, had a head concussion, or has been ill for several days.

So just how safe is soccer?

Many parents quietly push their children into playing soccer instead of football as a fall sport because they feel that their children run less of a risk of being seriously injured in soccer. But that sense of security may in fact just be a myth.

A recent study in the *British Journal of Sports Medicine* strongly indicates that the risk of injury in soccer "may have been played down."

Studying videotapes of international soccer matches, the study found that players had a 12 percent risk of injury in every game. More significantly, it was reported that almost one third of all professional players suffer at least one injury per season.

(Source: *The New York Times,* December 1, 1998)

Having a Medical Professional on the Sidelines

If one of the team parents happens to be a physician, nurse, or other health professional who is certified in emergency medical treatment, get to know this parent and see if he or she can be on hand for games (and perhaps even practices). Very few youth sports leagues require that a physician or nurse be in attendance for league games, but that doesn't mean that their presence won't be welcomed. On the off chance that an injury does require more than just a bag of ice or some medicine and bandages, you'll feel a lot better having a real medical pro in attendance who can immediately help out.

If you aren't trained in emergency medicine and aren't certain of the child's physical injury, be careful not to do anything that may actually cause more harm than good. Be especially careful with children who may have suffered head, neck, or spine injuries! Instead, call medical professionals — they'll be on the scene before you know it. In the meantime, do what you can to calm the child and reassure him or her that help is on the way.

Making Equipment a Priority

Sometimes, a child won't wear equipment because they don't want to. Other times, the parents aren't aware that the equipment is a requisite for play.

Most youth leagues have a standard ritual before each game in which the ref lines up both teams and personally checks to make sure that every player is wearing the proper gear: checking to make certain that every young athlete is wearing the proper shin guards, has a mouthpiece in place, or is wearing a protective cup, and so on. If the child isn't properly outfitted, the ref tells him and the coach that he can't play until the proper equipment is in place.

What about protective goggles?

If a youngster wears glasses (and lots of them do!), suggest to their parents that they may want to seriously look into having the child obtain a pair of protective goggles. Although lots of glasses have been designed to be safe, the vast majority of them aren't designed for use in heavy competition with a lot of contact.

Goggles provide the maximum amount of protection for all athletes who need glasses. Even though it may take the child a few days to get accustomed to the goggles, after awhile, most kids look on them as part of their uniform. Let parents know that these goggles do exist, and that they are worth investigating.

While this may be a pain in the neck for you as the coach, the truth is, it's a solid practice and should be encouraged. Be sure to check that your players are wearing the proper equipment for each game and practice. In addition to protecting the kids, checking for equipment in practice gets kids in the habit of putting on their gear, which will help them remember to bring it for the games.

Addressing Special Needs of Certain Kids

Besides injuries that occur during the course of competition, you may encounter other physical situations involving the players on your team. Asthma, for example, is a fairly common problem these days for kids. Some kids even bring inhalers to the games or practices so that, if they run short of breath, they can quickly turn to their medication. Many times, kids who suffer from asthma or other related breathing problems are supposed to use their inhalers even before the activity gets going. As the coach, you have to get up to speed on each child's condition so that you know from the parents how they want to you handle any concerns or flare-ups.

Common ailments include respiratory problems (such as asthma and allergies), diabetes, eyesight or vision concerns (wearing glasses or contact lens), special medications, infectious diseases, head lice, and so on. Ask the parents at the very first meeting (see Chapter 7) if their kids have any medical concerns that you should be aware of. (Make clear to the parents that they have a choice: They can either talk to you right then and there, or if they wish, due to confidentiality concerns, they can call you in private about their child's concerns.)

No matter how parents contact you, it is absolutely essential that you know whether the kids on your team have a particular medical problem — a problem that may affect the way they play or the way you coach them. That's not only fair to the child, it's also just common sense.

Chapter 14

Coaching Your Own Child

- -

In This Chapter

▶ Avoiding the appearance of favoritism

▶ Working with your child regardless of his or her ability

▶ Understanding the politics of choosing All-Star teams

- -

*M*ost parents assume that coaching their own kids on a youth sports team is a dream come true. What could be more fun than being able to share the experience of youth sports with your child by volunteering to be his or her coach?

Well, if you think coaching your own child on a youth sports team is going to be nothing more than a dream come true, here's your wake-up call. The truth is, while it can be a glorious experience for you, your child, and your child's teammates, you have to do a little planning before you sign up for your coach's whistle and clipboard.

Finding Out What Your Child Wants

The first step before deciding whether to coach your child is to ask your son or daughter for his or her input — no matter how young or old your child is, how much you want to coach your child, or how well you know the game's strategies and skills.

If you're seriously thinking about volunteering to coach your son or daughter's team, check first with your child several months before the season starts. Ask her directly whether she'd like you to coach her team in the upcoming season. Tell her that you think it'll be fun, but that you won't sign on if she feels that it will interfere with her enjoyment of the game, or for that matter, if she feels that she may have a problem at home with your serving as her parent *and* coach.

TIP

"I'm the star of this team . . . because my Mom is the coach!"

While most kids embrace the idea of having a mom or dad coach their team, many times they struggle when the first practice rolls around. Especially when kids are under the age of 10, young athletes often sense a feeling of entitlement because a parent is the head coach.

To counteract this attitude as well as to prevent it from happening in the first place, be clear right from the start that this kind of attitude isn't going to be tolerated. As you drive to practice or talk over dinner, patiently explain to your child why being the coach's kid doesn't entitle him or her to special treatment. If you have this conversation early, issues of favoritism and entitlement can be easily handled when they come up.

That's all you have to say. Even the youngest athlete will have a clear opinion of whether she wants her Mom or Dad to coach her and her friends. The good news is that, in most cases, your child will be absolutely thrilled that you want to coach her, and will give you a hearty thumbs-up.

TIP

If the child agrees that you should coach the team, however, you have to look your child in the eye and remind her that, as her coach, you won't be able to give her any special treatment or favoritism. You also expect her to follow all of the team rules, and she has to respond to you just like any other member of the team. This is difficult. While your child may understand that she isn't allowed to get any special treatment from you, when the season gets underway, she may quickly forget that edict and expect, in fact, to receive special treatment. This is why it's important to keep reminding your child as the season approaches that you have to coach all of the children in the same manner — with no exceptions.

HEADS UP

Being fair doesn't mean you have to be tougher or meaner with your own child. Some coaches do that. They feel that they have to push their own flesh-and-blood tougher, longer, and harder than the other kids in order to get greater performances. Don't make that mistake. If you do, your extra pushing and prodding may only result in pushing your child *out* of sports, rather than continuing in them.

Communicating with Your Child

Communicating with your child may be tougher than you think. Those who coach their own children openly acknowledge that having their children listen to and respond to constructive criticism can be quite challenging and perplexing. To get around this sticky situation, enlist the aid of an assistant coach to help get your message across to your youngster. All you have to say is something like the following:

"Say, Mike, can you do me a big favor? Keep an eye on David during the practice sessions. He really needs to pay some attention to his ballhandling and his conditioning, but I find that if I talk to him about these concerns, he's likely not to take it too seriously. So, if you would, perhaps you can chat with David, gain his trust, and encourage him. I find that he responds well to praise and encouragement, and if it comes from you, I think he'll respond for us in a big way."

That's all you have to say. Just make certain that the assistant coach doesn't turn into a drill sergeant on your child, so keep checking whether your child is responding in a positive fashion. Usually, because he or she is taking constructive criticism from a different coach, your child will take those comments more seriously than if they came from you.

Being Prepared for a Presumption of Favoritism

While you're focused on preparing a practice session or putting together a line-up for the game, you can often forget or overlook that some parents of the kids may be sitting as judge and jury on your ability as a coach.

This judging occurs whether you like it or not. You have to understand and accept the fact that every parent up in the stands or standing on the sidelines is quietly gauging how much playing time you're giving to their child, what position they're allowed to play, and how you're treating their little one on an individual basis. What is each parent's point of perspective? They're quietly comparing how their child is being treated in relation to your own.

This comparison may not be fair and it may not be right, but the truth is, it happens all the time. And if you show even the slightest bit of favoritism or preferential treatment to your child, chances are, you'll be the main topic of non-flattering discussion at dinner tables all over the neighborhood for that night and for weeks to come.

What kinds of coaching actions give the parents the impression that your child is getting preferential treatment? Consider the following:

✔ You put your child in the lineup first and play him in the most desired position (for example, he bats third and plays shortstop, plays center forward on the soccer team, gets to handle the ball all the time in basketball, and so on).

✔ As the head coach, you select which kids serve as captains of the team, and you just happen to select your child as one of the captains.

✔ You put your child up for selection as one of the team's candidates for the league's All-Star teams.

✔ Your child gets first choice of the best uniforms on the team, as well as his or her choice of their favorite number.

✔ You utilize your child as kind of an assistant coach — you ask her to help out and show the other kids how to do certain drills and skills ("Ann, why don't you show the rest of the team how you dribble the ball?").

Of course, this is just a small sampling of the kinds of actions that can lead to charges of preferential treatment. Keep in mind that no consideration is usually given by the other parents as to whether your child just happens to be the best athlete on the team or most deserving to be selected as captain or as an All-Star. While those are important considerations to you and your child, unfortunately, it's not often seen in that way by the other parents. In fact, many times the other parents may even suggest that "My kid would be an All-Star, too, if he got the same kind of favorite treatment that Coach gives his own kid."

As unfair as this conclusion may be to you and your son or daughter, this happens all the time. To allay these fears, bend over backward to make certain that these perceptions aren't allowed to fester. Here are some time-tested suggestions:

✔ **If your child is 11 or older and is clearly one of the better players on the team, talk with her about her talent and the responsibilities that come with that talent.** Explain to her that because she is one of the better athletes on the team, she must become a true leader — do more for the team than just score goals or earn points. Let her know that you're looking to her to give pats on the backs to the other players, encourage the other kids, and make certain that the team is cohesive. Let her know that you're personally looking to her to make your job as the coach that much easier.

Note that this is intended for kids 11 or older — with younger children, this kind of chat isn't necessary.

When your child rises to this challenge, praise her for being a good sport, doing the right thing, and making all the kids on the team feel important. By openly acknowledging (in a private session) to your child that she is a terrific player, you've already made her feel good about herself and her ability. And by introducing a little more leadership responsibility into her life, you've also taken her to a new level — that of becoming sensitive to her teammates and their needs. That's a major step forward in the maturation of any child.

✔ **Keep a scoresheet (see Chapter 10 and Appendix B) in which you keep track of where everybody played during the game or meet and how much playing time they received.** If necessary, when in doubt, if it means keeping the peace with your team, give your own child *less* playing time than the others.

Isn't that unfair to your child? Yes, of course it is. But in the long run, you'll have an easier time pointing out to parents that your own child is getting less playing time than theirs.

✔ **Make certain that you rotate all of your players during the game, match, or meet.** This may appease any parents who may think that your child is playing the preferred position(s). Point to the scoresheet in case of any parental confrontations, and be certain to keep all of your scoresheets from the entire season.

If the season breaks into two parts, for example, the fall and the spring, keep your scoresheets from the fall right through the spring season. After the year is finally done and your team has finished its season, you can finally put the scoresheets aside.

Watching Your Words Carefully — with All Kids!

As the head coach, watching what you say and how you say it is of supreme importance. Remember that your team is composed of all different kinds of kids, and each one has his or her own way of responding to your coaching technique. And of course, you have the double responsibility of not only coaching all the other kids on the team, but your child as well. You want to be very careful that you leave a solid impression on all the children, but especially on your own child.

You can never go wrong with offering praise. Kids like praise and respond to it — and their parents like it, too. And guess what? Your son or daughter likes to hear praise as well. Just because you're the coach doesn't mean that you're not allowed to praise your own child.

The basic underlying theme of coaching is education — your job is to teach the children. Scolding them for being out of position, for not knowing the rules of the game, or for not playing up to their potential is *not* teaching. It's just venting. Your task is not to point out the child's mistakes or miscues. All athletes make mistakes — that's part of all games. Rather, your job is to educate them and persuade them that they can correct their errors, and even better, that perhaps they can work to prevent them from happening in the future.

When your child is one of the weaker athletes on the team

Sometimes your child is one of the younger kids on the squad, is physically smaller than the other kids, or just isn't very good in the sport. If your child is happy to be on the team and understands his limitations, your only job is to encourage him and applaud his efforts, just as you would with any other child on the team.

Do you ever tell your child that he or she isn't as good as another player? Of course not! There's no reason for you to compare one player against another, and you want to be particularly delicate with your own child. Let your child — along with the other kids on the team — find out how good (or not so good) he is in his own way. Nobody had to explain to you when you were a kid what your talent and potential was. That's the beauty of athletic competition: All youngsters eventually find out for themselves just how much talent they truly have.

The younger the kids, the more mistakes they're going to make. That's what all kids do in sports, they make mistakes — even your own child! It's your job to teach them how to learn from those mistakes. The trick is in not overreacting, but rather in trying to encourage all the kids (including your child) to come back strong and bounce back in a positive way from their mistakes.

And even if you're just kidding, you can get into trouble when you use sarcasm with kids or if your comments are perceived as being too gruff or harsh. Not only will that player not respond to your admonitions, but he or she is going to be less inclined to play hard in the future. Kids usually only like to perform well for coaches who appreciate their efforts.

Compare the two following approaches after a team of 9- and 10-year-olds have just lost a soccer game 4 to 1. After the post-game ritual of shaking the other team's hands, the coach brings the kids together for a post-game chat. As you read through each coach's postmortem of the game, ask yourself which approach would best work for your child:

Coach A: "Kids, I know you're disappointed with the outcome today. So am I. But what's particularly frustrating to me is that you're making so many mistakes out there that it's difficult to keep track. Too many giveaways to the other team. Not enough pressure being applied to their attackers. We're out of position. Lousy throw-ins. Not enough hustle. In short, the other team wanted to win this game a lot more than we did, and I don't think there's one kid on our team who played their very best game. So, keep this loss in mind, and think about it, and what you did wrong today. Then, when we practice next week, come prepared to work hard."

Coach B: "Kids, I know you're disappointed with the outcome today. So am I. But let's give the other team some credit. They played one of their very best games today and the results showed. Now, I think we also played hard. But we did make some mistakes along the way. The good news is that, with a little work, we can easily correct and prevent these mistakes from happening again. And that's what we'll want to work on in practice next week. Yes, we still need work on knowing our positions on our throw-ins, and in applying pressure to the other team.

"But on the other hand, we also made some fine plays today. We had some sharp passes, and some excellent shots on goal. So, forget this one, because it's over. Let's look ahead to next week, and work on preparing for that one."

Which coach would you prefer to be? Who do you think your kid would respond to? Do you think parents would prefer Coach A or Coach B for their children? Think about this question, because it will go a long way in determining your coaching style and the impact you leave on the kids on your team.

Understanding the Politics of All-Star Teams

Does this sound familiar? "Look, son, I'm sorry you didn't make the All-Star team this year. You see, making that team has more to do with, uh, league politics than it does with talent."

Ahh — politics. That's the catch-all in most towns when sports go wrong.

Taking advantage of road trips to bond with your child

Many youth teams play "away" games, either against neighboring towns or during a weekend tournament. If you and your child find yourself going on the road, look upon this time together as a wonderful way to really bond with your child.

To get your child to open up during these trips, start the conversation by asking him about his best experiences playing sports, who his favorite player or team is, or what his favorite drill in practice is. Flatter him. Get him to start talking about himself and that will get him going. And after your child starts chatting, just follow his lead.

Before long, as you make your way to the road game, you'll find that your child is beginning to look at you in a different way — not just as a parent, but as a real coach — a coach he can truly talk to.

Unfortunately, few 12-year-olds understand what the word "politics" means, much less how it affects their dreams of making the local All-Star team. *Politics,* of course, is the term that parents and coaches employ when they feel that an injustice has been done, either to their child's team or more significantly, to their child.

Suppose the league wants three kids from each team to make the All-Star team. To do that, many head coaches will simply choose the three best players on their teams. That's where the friction can begin, because parents rarely agree with the coach's selections, and things can really get out of hand if the coach happens to choose his own kid as an All-Star.

When selecting All-Star teams in your town or the All-Star members of your team, here's a solid suggestion: Explain to the kids that because it's their league and their All-Star team, they ought to select their All-Stars. To accomplish this, allow the kids to vote for three players from their team to be All-Stars — and yes, they can vote for themselves. The voting should be private, using the pencil and paper approach. More often than not, kids quickly recognize which of their peers are the more talented players. Even better, any accusations of "favoritism" or "politics" disappears; after all, the parents and coaches didn't choose the teams — the kids did!

Be wary of selecting All-Star teams when the kids are very young. Children under the age of 10 or 11 have a difficult time understanding why they aren't chosen for an All-Star team. For those who do make the team, it's a nice boost to their (and to their parent's) ego, but think about all of the other kids who had hoped to make the team, only to see their dreams squashed. That really isn't the purpose of youth sports teams — to discourage or disappoint kids who enjoy playing sports.

Be wary of your league when they want to put together All-Star teams for younger children. Ask the league how the teams are selected, and be certain to ask why it's so essential that they even have an All-Star team for kids who are younger than 11.

Chapter 15

Dealing with the Stresses of the Job

*W*hen you volunteer to serve as the head coach of a youth sports team, you're actively placing yourself in a role that you may not be accustomed to. Because you serve in a position of some authority within the community's sports hierarchy, you put yourself right in the line of fire.

Being a coach brings with it a certain set of responsibilities: obligations that include doing the right thing for the kids, for their parents, and for yourself and your family. And while these responsibilities may seem somewhat tame (for example, making sure the kids all play, maintaining a sense of sportsmanship, behaving oneself on the sidelines, and so forth), the truth is that in America today, youth sports coaches — especially those who don't live up to these obligations — often find themselves and their reputations embroiled in controversy in their respective communities.

Congratulations, Coach — You're the Topic of Saturday Night Conversations!

Saturday night get-togethers of parents and neighbors are usually the breeding grounds for sessions of dissension. Parents sometime chat with more emotion and inner heat about a child's playing time than about who's going to be the next President of the United States or even how the local pro or college team is doing.

From coast to coast and everywhere in between, typical discussions center on topics such as the following:

- ✔ "What does he (the coach) think he's doing? I hear him yell and scream at the kids a lot more than I would like."

- ✔ "She (the coach) is really becoming an embarrassment, the way she's always sniping and barking at the refs all game long. Even the kids don't like it."

- ✔ "Why doesn't he just let the Johnson kid play and score? I mean it's clear he's our best player, and if he played where he could score, the entire team would benefit."

- ✔ "I don't think it's fair that he always puts my daughter on the second line of players. She never gets a chance to play with the better kids on the team."

And on and on it goes. In some respects, these impromptu sessions among parents serve as good therapy, because they allow the parents to express their frustrations and disappointments regarding their children's sports careers among their own adult friends and peers.

Rarely is it noted, by the way, that perhaps the coach isn't at fault, but rather that the child's lack of physical ability or motivational desire to improve their skills is the culprit!

Working effectively with unhappy parents

Most parents watch their kids only during the games — they don't observe their children during practice sessions. That's too bad because during the practice sessions (and not necessarily during a game) is when the coach makes judgments about each child's ability to play the sport, and how much the child really enjoys being there.

Every parent watches his child in the most optimistic way possible — only the rare parent can objectively analyze just how good (or not so good) his child is as compared to the other kids in her peer group. This, by the way, is only natural. As the coach, expect parents to feel this way about their kids. But just because parents see their kids as being one of the more gifted athletes on your team, doesn't mean that their perception matches reality. As such, youth coaches are often confronted by a concerned parent who, in effect, wants to know how come you don't recognize that his child is certainly one of the premier players on the team.

Here's a typical conversation:

> Parent: "Coach, just a quick observation: It seems to me that if you put my son Mickey on the front line with Bobby and Timmy, the team would be scoring a lot more goals."
>
> Coach (knowing in her heart that Bobby and Timmy are excellent players, but the boy in question — Mickey — is a couple of steps behind them): "Well, I actually thought of doing that, but I feel I ought to spread out the talent in a balanced way on the team. That's why I have your Mickey on the second line. It just gives us a much more potent attack."
>
> Parent: "I understand, but maybe just a couple of times in the game you could put Mickey with the two other talented boys. Otherwise, Mickey is always stuck playing with the other kids, and I think his skills are suffering because he's not playing on that first line."
>
> Coach: "I see your point. Well, I'll tell you what — I'm not making any promises, but I'll see what I can do."

The coach in this confrontation has handled the parent's concerns: She allows the parent to make his point about his child playing with the team's best players, and has an intelligent answer in response. When the parent asks about Mickey getting some playing time with Bobby and Timmy, the coach is smart enough to acknowledge the parent's suggestion, take it under advisement, and go from there.

If you use this approach, make a mental note to ensure that Mickey does, in fact, play a few shifts with Bobby and Timmy together. While that may not totally satisfy the parent, at least it shows the parent that you're listening and trying to accommodate his needs.

Avoiding the cold, honest truth

Some coaches feel that the best approach is simply to be direct, even blunt, with the parent.

Here are two examples:

> "Look, the team plays better with your son playing where he is. Besides, it wouldn't be fair to the others just to single out your child and give him preferential treatment."
>
> "The truth is, Mr. Jones, that your child isn't as talented as some of the other kids on the team, and as such, he doesn't deserve to play on the first line with the other two boys."

Yikes! While both of these answers are direct, to the point, and may carry more than a grain of truth, they are both insensitive to the parent standing before you.

Before you take it upon yourself to tell a meddling parent what you really think of his child, keep in mind that anything you say in front of a parent may be used against you in the community in which you coach. In other words, always keep your patience and be diplomatic at all times! Unless you're planning on moving out of town within the next few weeks, your words may follow you around town like a bad debt. Before you know it, your name — and reputation — will be sullied and soiled.

Even worse, your disgraced name will be on the lips of every parent in your neighborhood. Carpool gossip, dinner-time conversations, and cocktail parties will begin with one parent saying to another:

> "Did you hear what Coach said about Joe and Mary Morris's boy? She came right out and told Joe that his son wasn't very good and that he sure didn't deserve more playing time."

> "That's absolutely disgraceful! Where does that coach come off where she can insult a parent about his child? Besides, I've seen the coach's own kid play, and he's certainly no superstar. But that doesn't stop the coach from seeing to it that her own kid gets plenty of playing time."

> "You know, if I were that parent, I would complain directly to the league's board of directors about the coach. I mean, how can the league allow such insensitive cementheads to be around our kids? It's just not fair! It's supposed to be about letting the kids play and have fun — not some sort of ego trip for the coach to have a winning record."

Of course, it makes no difference that the coach isn't there to defend herself and her reputation, or for that matter, to explain what "really" happened when the parent confronted her about a child's playing time. Not only won't the coach have a chance to defend herself, nobody is even slightly interested in hearing a rebuttal. All they want to do is join in the verbal lynch mob and unload their own anger regarding the coach.

Even worse, the parents start telling their kids on the team to start being wary about the coach, even instructing the kids to "make sure and tell Mom and Dad if the coach says something to you that's mean or less than encouraging." In other words, the parents start making the kids a bit suspicious about the coach. This becomes a nasty situation for all involved.

Calling an emergency team meeting

What, as a coach, do you do if any of the following situations occur?

- ✔ You find that you're getting fewer and fewer kids attending your practice sessions.
- ✔ You discover that, midway through the season, there's a lessening of enthusiasm on the team.
- ✔ You get the definite sense that some of the parents are less friendly toward you than they were at the start of the season.

From situations like these, you're probably getting a distinct sense that things are beginning to get out of hand and are starting to slide downhill with your team. If so, the time has come for an emergency team meeting.

An *emergency team meeting* with parents should be brief, to the point, and ideally, a chance for you to clear the air — not only from your perspective, but also from the parents'.

In most cases, you'll have a better meeting if only the moms and dads attend this emergency team meeting. In fact, let the parents know that you think it's a good idea if their kids aren't there. Also, be certain that you give plenty of notice as to when the meeting is going to take place. Let parents know that you need them in attendance!

1. After the parents arrive, you run the meeting.

Try to minimize the tension in the air by smiling and exhibiting a calm and professional attitude.

2. Start off the meeting by discussing why you called the meeting.

You can and should be direct about the issues that have popped up, but be careful not to mention any names of players. Furthermore, avoid pointing accusing fingers of blame. The last thing you want to do is enrage the parents even more.

3. Have your few words prepared and get to your point quickly.

Be brief. Speak for no more than 5 minutes — tops! You can then open the floor to any parents who may have questions.

If the parents feel somewhat skittish about asking a question directly, bring along a number of index cards and pencils in which the moms and dads can write down their questions on the cards, and then hand them to you without being signed.

Whatever process you employ, keep the meeting moving along quickly, and make certain that any parent who wants to say something has a chance to say it.

Don't feel compelled to answer every comment or criticism. That's not going to be very productive for anybody. In addition, don't believe that you're going to walk away from this meeting having convinced every parent there that you really are a great coach. That's a nice aspiration to have, but the truth is, it's just not going to happen. Rather, the realistic goal for these types of meetings is to state your concerns and give the parents a chance to make their concerns known to you.

Here's a typical example: As the coach, you have been extraordinarily conscientious at making sure that every kid on the team gets equal playing time, regardless of their ability. Of course, you're also the first to recognize that by giving each kid equal time on the field — regardless of their ability — the team has probably lost more games than it would have if you had given the majority of the playing time to more athletically gifted kids on the team.

You make this philosophy clear to the parents at the emergency team meeting. But as soon as you ask for feedback from the parents, one mom pipes up and says, "I don't think it's right that our team loses games because you purposely let all the kids have equal playing time. My own son comes home in tears whenever the team loses, and he's doubly upset because he knows the team could have won if you hadn't taken out the best players." Another parent may add, "Yeah, I agree. Why do you insist on equal playing time for the kids? No other team in the league does that, so why are our kids punished because of your antiquated views?"

After a few more comments along these lines, you can stop the discussion and simply say to the parents, "Okay, if I'm hearing you correctly, what you're telling me is that you prefer that I coach the team to win, and win only — regardless of which kids play. Is that right? But you also understand that some of the kids — perhaps your own child — may get a lot less playing time because of this new policy. Does everybody understand this?"

Framed in that light, you may find that some of the other parents (especially the parents of the less gifted kids) saying, "Now, wait a minute. I'm pretty happy with the fact that my child gets to play a lot. Coach, if you decide to play to win, only a handful of kids are going to benefit from that new philosophy."

Exactly! So, the issue of "playing to win versus everybody plays" becomes an issue not so much for you to decide, but rather for all the team parents to determine. You can easily coach either way. You merely need some direction from the parents.

This is what the emergency team meeting is designed to accomplish. As the coach, you take on the role of the team mediator, not a dictator. You make it clear to the parents that you are there to serve them and their children, and you'll gladly coach according to their wishes, so long as their wishes are the consensus and that the wishes make sense.

Listening to Your "Coaching Partner" — Your Spouse

When you volunteer to coach in your community, you're not coaching in a vacuum. Your spouse may be party to the microscopic eye of the team parents. But rather than chafe at this backdoor gossipfest, you can actually grow from what your spouse hears about you and your coaching style. Pay attention to what your husband or wife hears on the sidelines, in a grocery store, or waiting at the school bus stop. Too many coaches simply insist that they "don't have time for idle gossip," but the truth is, your spouse is probably going to be in the center of it all.

Almost no one ever goes up to the coach's spouse and blurts out, "Your husband (wife) is one lousy coach!" Instead, the insinuations and comments tend to be much more subtle in scope, but they are still quite cutting. It's up to the coach's spouse to hear the inflection and tone of these comments carefully in order to understand what's really being said. That is, your spouse can add some very valuable insight as to how you are being perceived by the parents.

Here are some examples (along with translations):

> "Coach certainly gets very excited during the games. I hope he doesn't have any blood pressure problems." (Translation: The parents think that you're too loud when coaching the games.)

> "Well, our coach seems to be learning the game right along with the kids." (Translation: The parents don't think you know the rules or strategies of the game.)

> "Did you notice how well organized and disciplined that opposing team's coach was today? He was very impressive." (Translation: How come we don't have a coach like that?)

> "I feel sorry for our coach. She puts all that time and effort into coaching, but the kids just aren't playing well for her." (Translation: The parents don't think you're a very good coach if you work so hard at it and the kids still don't win!)

On occasion, your spouse may become so emotionally outraged by what's overheard that he or she is tempted to lash out and throttle someone. While that reaction is understandable, you both have to also understand that it's simply not acceptable. Getting into a shouting match with a parent is unbelievably counter-productive. Nobody wins the argument. Even worse, you've now made an enemy for life, and beyond that, what do you say to your own child when she asks you why you're mad at her friend's father or mother?

When coping with neighborhood gossip about your coaching abilities, muster up the inner strength to listen to it (or whatever your spouse brings back to you), but don't ever give in to it. Gossip usually starts because somebody feels that he has been shortchanged or gypped or because he is downright angry. And if another person will give him the opportunity to express his feelings, that angry person will — as gossip.

Giving Yourself a Job Evaluation

At the end of the season, you owe it to yourself (and to your family) to honestly evaluate just how well you did your job. Give yourself a week or so to let the season settle in before you start reviewing whether you enjoyed the experience and whether you'd like to do it again next year. Most importantly, go back and ask your child whether he or she enjoyed having you serve as the coach.

And don't be afraid to do a survey of your team. Provide a quick — and anonymous — survey sheet that the kids (and their parents) can use to evaluate your work as a coach. Make sure their names aren't on the evaluations (so they can be honest in their critiques).

Keep the survey short. Sample questions may include the following:

- ✔ Did you (or your child) get enough playing time?
- ✔ Did you (or your child) improve your skills?
- ✔ Did you (or your child) have fun this season?

You may want to provide a space at the bottom of the page where the children or their parents can make some general observations and comments.

For most coaches, this kind of evaluation is good news. But even if you discover some negative comments (for example, "Coach yells too much" or "Coach doesn't give enough praise"), you can use this tool to improve your own coaching skills.

Volunteering to help out as a coach is a wonderful experience, and it gives you more of an opportunity to bond with your child during precious developing years. Even better, especially if you've had concerns about the volunteer coaches who have worked with your child in the past, being the coach affords you the opportunity to make sure your child and their friends have a terrific time.

On the other hand, if you find the season to be a difficult one — perhaps you underestimated the time commitment, found that your priorities for the team didn't match up with the parents', or discovered that you had some problems keeping your emotions in check — you can look upon the past season as a personal learning experience. If nothing else, you'll come away with a healthier respect for the work of coaches and how difficult it really is to work with children on a weekly basis.

Never think of a tough season as a disapointment. Just rack it up as an experience that you were glad to at least have had the chance to do it, and then move on from there.

Presenting Final Words of Praise

But before you hang up your whistle and clipboard for the season, it is incumbent on you to go to every child on your team and give each one some words of specific praise. You can do this at the last practice session, but if your team has a team party (and most youth teams do), you have a golden opportunity to make every kid feel that he or she is special and unique.

Of course, not every child is going to have been a superstar player on your team. That's not the point. As the coach, you have to find at least two or three specific and positive comments or anecdotes about each child as they come forward to receive their certificates or trophies or whatever the league provides for all the kids. This does take some preparation and planning, and if you want, you can note your individual comments on an index card. But whatever you say about each member of your team, make sure that your comments are full of praise, that they are specific to each child, and that you lead the applause.

The following is an example:

> "I just want you all to know what a special team player Susan is. A few weeks ago, when we were playing the Dragons, one of Susan's teammates accidentally brought the wrong jersey to the game. Susan's teammate thought that she wouldn't be able to play. But Susan — without any prodding from me or anybody else — quickly volunteered to share her jersey when she wasn't playing in the game just so her teammate wouldn't be left out. Sure enough, whenever Susan came out of the game, she and her teammate quickly ducked behind a tree so that Susan could share her jersey. Folks, that to me is the pure essence of teamwork, and I just want to take this moment to salute Susan for her unselfishness. She's the essence of a real team player."

Note that the coach never mentioned whether Susan scored any goals, or for that matter, was very good in the sport. Of course he can add all that into his speech, but by punctuating his talk with a specific anecdote of what a great team player Susan is, he has made his point in a big way. And that's the kind of positive impact a coach can have.

By the way, if you can arrange it, see if one of the moms or dads can have a camera ready so that each member of your team has their photo taken with you. Make certain you get two copies — one for you and one for the child. That makes for a wonderful keepsake for both you and each member of the team.

Make sure you take the time to thank all of the key team parents and your assistant coaches for a job well done. It's the rare youth coach who handles all of the coaching chores by herself, so before you start introducing the kids and talking about their season, salute the moms and dads who were there all season to help you, whether they made phone calls because of inclement weather or helped out with the mid-game or post-meet snacks and drinks.

Part V
The Part of Tens

The 5th Wave   By Rich Tennant

"I see Officer Ruiz is coaching the girls youth soccer team this year."

In this part . . .

This part gives you ten tips for parenting young athletes and thirty ways to become a great coach. Stop here for quick tidbits that only take a minute to digest.

Chapter 16

Ten Things Every Parent Should Know

In This Chapter

▶ Letting your child develop at his or her own pace

▶ Sharing in your child's joy without overdoing it

▶ Praising your child instead of criticizing

Much to the chagrin of many parents, close to 80 percent of all kids quit playing organized sports by the time they reach the age of 13. Many kids just leave on their own, realizing that, while perhaps playing sports is nice, their true interests (and talents) in life lie elsewhere. That's certainly understandable. But sadly, too many children quit because they're just burned out, feel too much parental pressure, or just don't see sports as being that much fun anymore. It's those kids, as a coach and parent, that you don't want to lose.

Give Your Child Some Space

It's not often discussed in coaching circles, but in much the same way that some moms and dads have a difficult and emotional time when their little one goes off to school for the first time, a parent can also have a somewhat difficult time when they entrust their little athlete to a youth league coach. In coping with this transition, a parent may stand on the sidelines and watch every second and every minute of every practice (as well as every game) just to make sure that his or her child is doing well on the team and that the coach is treating the child fairly.

This is certainly a fine intention, but what the parent may not realize is that the child is embarrassed by this overzealous attention to her individual athletic development. Always having mom or dad at every practice, watching the child's every move, and then talking in detail with your child about her progress in the car on the way home may set the stage for oversaturation — the child may begin to rebel against all of this attention being focused on her.

While it's great that you're there to cheer and root your child, it's also essential that you give her some psychological space. Give her the freedom to be on her own, to develop her own personality with her teammates and coach. Nobody likes having anyone look over her shoulder all the time — and that especially applies to your own child.

Give Your Child's Coach Some Space, Too

Just as your child most likely doesn't want you watching every move she makes on the practice field, the same goes for the coach. Give the coach some freedom to run his own practices and games.

If you have the time to watch and observe every practice and game, what's preventing you from helping out? Most youth teams are desperate to have parents help out as coaches or as assistant coaches — why not volunteer your services? Just keep in mind that if you do become an assistant coach, you have to focus your attention on all the kids on the team, not just your own.

Be There To Watch Your Child Compete

Show your support to the team and your child by attending as many games as you can. Most kids still get a big thrill out of having mom or dad at their games — and what they really want to hear after the game is how you enjoyed a particularly good play they made during a game.

Here are some examples:

> "Say, Sam, that was some steal you made in the third quarter — tell me about it."

> "Samantha, you played great today. What was your favorite play?"

The best way to share the moment with your kids is to let them do all the talking. You can get them going with some praise about their play, but let them take it from there.

Praise Your Child

When in doubt as to what to say, praise your child. This universal coaching truism applies to all kids, no matter what their ages or abilities. A child may have struck out three times in the game, but if he gets a hit on his fourth at-bat, that's all he wants to hear about. He may appear to be grumpy after the game because of his three strike-outs, but this is when you can really make a difference in that child's life.

Here's an example:

"Hey, that was some hit you got in that last at-bat. You really smoked that pitch!"

"Yeah, I guess so."

"So how come the sad attitude?"

"I struck out three times before that hit. Didn't you see that?"

"Well, sure, but everybody in baseball strikes out. There isn't a player anywhere who hasn't struck out. That's not what is important. What is important is that you rallied yourself and came back to get a solid hit."

"You really think so?"

"Of course! Sports is all about not giving up, and coming back for more. And that's just what you did! So tell me, what kind of pitch did you hit?"

While this entire conversation may last no more than three minutes, it can make a tremendous difference to a youngster. Communicate with him by using a little praise to get him going, and then sit back and let him do the talking.

Expose Your Kids To a Variety of Sports

So much attention is paid these days about the age at which a child should specialize in a sport. In some cases, parents actually chose a sport for their youngster instead of allowing the child to choose for him- or herself.

As a parent, it's your job to expose your child to as many different sports as possible when he's growing up. Bear in mind that this is no easy task because you have dozens of sports to choose from, including football, wrestling, figure skating, snowboarding — and everything in between.

But you aren't going to know which sport your kids are going to fall in love with until they've had a chance to try several. That's your responsibility — let them try as many as possible and follow where their hearts take them.

Should you have your child specialize in one sport?

Lots of top athletes today played more than one sport growing up. American League star outfielder Ben Grieve played soccer, basketball, and baseball. Jackie Joyner-Kersee was a top basketball player and sprinter. Tom Glavine was terrific in ice hockey and baseball. So was Larry Walker.

Major league baseball star Darin Estad, who grew up playing a number of sports in North Dakota, says "I feel kind of sorry for those kids who just play one sport growing up, then in the off-season all they do is exercise to improve the muscles you use for that one sport."

(Source: *Sports Illustrated,* 1998)

Let Them Develop Their Own Passion

Just because you grew up loving football, baseball, or basketball doesn't mean that your son or daughter is going to love those sports. You may discover that your child really gets turned on by sports that you never even heard of when you were a kid — mountain biking, snowboarding, speedskating, water polo, and so on.

Yes, you may feel a little disappointment or frustration in having to get acquainted with a sport that's totally foreign to you, but if you want to be a good sports parent or coach, allow your child to chase his or her passion. That's your child's choice — not yours.

Go Easy Down Memory Lane

If you were an athlete of sorts when you were a kid, you're going to be tempted to go down memory lane and enthrall your child with stories of how you scored the big touchdown or made the big play when you were growing up. For example: "Hey, did I ever tell you about the time I ran back a kickoff 93 yards?" or "Let me tell you about the time I scored 23 points in a playoff game."

While your child may enjoy hearing these memories occasionally, try to keep them in check: Such stories often leave the child with the impression that he or she has to reach a certain standard in order to gain your approval. This subtle form of parental pressure is probably the last impression you want to leave on your child, but unfortunately it can have that impact.

Try this approach: Every so often, before your child goes to bed at night, ask her if she remembers the time she scored her first goal in a soccer game, got the big hit, or had some other special moment in sports. Let her relive that wonderful memory for herself. Those are the memories that you want to leave with them — instead of unintentionally boring them with your own sports memories.

Be Careful About Applying Pressure

Very few parents bluntly tell their children, "Listen, I expect you to be the star of your team, and as such, I demand that you practice harder and work longer."

Rather, parents tend to apply pressure to their young athletes in more subtle ways, and in most cases, the pressure is unintended. But the pressure still exists, and your child picks up on it. As a parent, try to listen to yourself when you're talking sports with your child. See if you can take a step back and listen to the tone of your comments and suggestions. Try to evaluate whether you're subtly putting too much pressure on your child to succeed in sports.

How many times have you heard a pro athlete say about when he was growing up: "My parents really didn't put any pressure on me to play. They just let me go out and have fun."

That's not just a cliché. It's true. Perhaps there's a lesson in that for all sports parents.

Remember That It's Their Childhood, Not Yours

Your childhood is over. It's history. It's in the books, and it's not going to change, no matter how hard you try to push yourself — or your kid. Parents can forget this simple reality, and as a result, feel tempted to try and guide their children past the obstacles that they faced when they were growing up.

But when parents do this, they're overlooking one important element: Their child is not them. Children have their own agendas, their own dreams, their own ideas of what's cool and what isn't. And no matter how much parents try to push or prod them, eventually kids are going to do what they want to do.

That's the essence of growing up — not just in sports — but in life. Youngsters eventually reach adolescence and young adulthood, and then find their own way in the world. Parents are there to help guide them, but ultimately they're going to seek their *own* goals — not necessarily yours.

Remember when you were growing up, and how much fun you used to have playing sports? Well, here's some advice: Let your child have that same opportunity. Give them the kind of opportunity and freedom in much the same way that your parents gave you.

Let Them Dream

Chances are, nobody ever told you that you weren't good enough to play in the NBA or the NFL or for the Dodgers. Chances are, you figured that out for yourself when you were in high school or junior high. This is part of a maturation process called *self selection*, in which kids discover for themselves where their talents lie — in sports, music, theater, art, and so on. It's just part of growing up.

The process of self selection in sports happens all the time, and it's totally natural and to be expected. The vast majority of kids are smart enough to determine that they aren't blessed with the physical gifts to be able to compete at the sport's highest levels. They don't need parents to tell them that they're too small or too slow to ever become a professional athlete.

But all that being said, don't be in a rush to burst your child's dream of playing in the big leagues. Everyone — and especially your child — is allowed to dream. That's what propels adults and kids to higher levels of achievement. So as a caring parent or coach, let the kids dream their dreams.

But in the meantime, just in case they don't become the next Derek Jeter, Michael Jordan, or Venus or Serena Williams, just make certain that they do their homework. That's what you can — and should — insist on.

Chapter 17

Ten Great Coaching Tips

*T*o give you a brief recap of the major coaching points in this book, or if you just want to review the basic essentials of what's involved in volunteering to coach a youth team, here are ten tips to help ensure that you and the kids you coach enjoy the upcoming season.

Of course, every coach is unique in his approach to the sport, the kids on the team, and his outlook toward the season, but you can use these guidelines as a starting point to help keep you focused on the right priorities when coaching and teaching young athletes.

Be Sensitive to Every Child's Needs

When you receive your team's roster, look at the names of the kids who have been assigned to your team. Some of them you may already know; others will be kids who you most likely have never met before. But within a few weeks, it's your first responsibility to not only know each child on your team, but to have developed a real rapport with each one.

You do that by learning their names, recognizing their faces, and talking with each child during practice. As they go through their drills, watch them carefully — not only in terms of their skill development, but also in how they react with the other kids on the team: Do they have lots of friends on the squad or do they stand off to the side? Are they smiling and cheery or are they tentative and unsure of themselves? Bit by bit, you'll get a better understanding of how each child is interacting with the rest of the team.

In order to start making conversation with shy players, ask them who their favorite pro players or teams are. If they're so shy that they don't care to form an opinion on that, ask which positions are their favorites. If you're still having difficulty, try applying some simple praise.

Here are two examples:

> "Jane, it looks to me like you run pretty fast, so I'm going to play you in a position where speed is important. How does that sound to you?"

> "I'll tell you what, Mike, you're a big, strong kid, so I want to use your size as a natural force. How about if we try you in a position where you can really utilize your weight as a strength?"

The key is being sensitive to the child's personality and his or her needs. Praise is a wonderful way to gain their attention, and you can build from there. Most importantly, get each child to the point where he or she feels comfortable talking with you. Make your team feel as though they're truly a part of your life. Treat all the kids in such a way that they're involved in the team — never exclude anybody or make any player feel as though they're being left out or forgotten.

Get the Kids to Believe in Themselves

It's not enough that your team has developed, or is developing, some physical skills. The kids also have to have someone who allows them to believe in themselves.

Self confidence is a magical potion for everyone, but it's particularly potent for youngsters who are involved in sports. You have to use lots and lots of sincere praise to help each child develop enough courage and self-confidence to venture forth and try their best in athletic competitions.

You may encounter kids who, if anything, have too much self-confidence to the point of being too cocky. But most children, especially when they become frustrated or flustered occasionally in a sport, look for guidance, sympathy, and a helping hand when they make up their mind that they want to progress. That's where you, as the coach, can have a major impact.

Don't Let Noisy Parents Get out of Control

Sadly, you're probably going to have one or two parents of kids on your team who are going to push the limit on game day to the point of being loud, obnoxious, and at times, just plain poor sports.

As the coach, you have to walk a fine line. On one hand, you aren't there to govern the actions or behaviors of one of the adults attending the game. But by the same token, you do have a responsibility to the kids on the team to set the right example.

Here's a rule to guide you: If it's clear to you that the offending parent is giving the festivities a bad taste, it's also clear to all in attendance at the game that something ought to be done. Don't wait for the ref or official or ump to do something. Rather, if you suspect a problem is brewing, nip it in the bud.

You can handle this in several ways, but the most effective — and safest — way to handle such a problem parent is to tell them in a reassuring but firm tone that "It's really not fair to the kids or to the ref that you're making so much noise." Most parents — even the obnoxious ones — will calm down after being addressed by you, the coach. Just make certain that you go over and address the parent in a cheerful manner, and don't be confrontational.

If the problem persists, see if you can chat with the parent after the game. Let him or her know that the league really doesn't want any problems with unruly behavior, and that as the team coach, you're under some pressure to keep the league rules in effect. If that doesn't work, you have every right to report the parent to the league officials.

Most leagues have rules on their books that banish unruly parents from the games. In some leagues, the ref or official has the ultimate right to stop any game and demand that the unruly parent leave. Hopefully, these situations won't occur when you're coaching, but sadly, you have to be prepared in case they do.

Cooperate with Officials

Forget trying to play psychological games on the officials. Some youth coaches fully believe in "working over" the refs the way that some professional coaches do, in the hopes of gaining some sort of edge over close calls.

But the truth is — this tactic really doesn't work at the youth level! If anything, it will likely backfire on you and your team as the ref will be offended by your abrasive behavior. Besides, if you're at the point where you truly feel you have to "work over" the officials so that your team can prevail, you're taking youth league coaching much too seriously.

If you want to make a favorable impression on the ref, just do the right thing. Be pleasant and gracious, and exhibit good sportsmanship at all times — even when a close call goes against your team. Officials are people, too, and they fully appreciate the coach who treats them with respect and dignity. And who knows? Because you're perceived by the ref as a "good guy," maybe the next close call will go your way.

Be Careful When Trying Reverse Psychology on a Child

Too many youth coaches see themselves as being amateur sports psychologists. They see a kid with a bundle of talent but who doesn't seem to work hard, so the coach immediately tries an old-fashioned home remedy of "reverse psychology."

"Hey, Mikey, here's the deal. It's pretty clear that you have the talent to play this game, but you just don't want to hustle. So you know what? Why don't you just quit, because we just haven't got time for quitters here."

That's a pretty strong dose of reverse psychology. And who knows — maybe if you're a professional coach and you're working with a 24-year-old pro athlete who's loafing, such an approach may just work. But with a kid — say an 8- or 11-year-old — such an approach will likely not work. In fact, it may backfire and the child really will quit — because he thinks that you want him to. And if that happens, you have a lot of explaining to do to the child's parents and to the child.

Reverse psychology can be a potent weapon. Just be careful of how you apply it.

Forget the Knute Rockne Pep Talks

Young kids don't need to get psyched up for a big game. They don't need you to help them get focused on the event. They come to play, and they usually play hard because it's fun. So skip the motivational pep talks. Instead, just concentrate on telling the kids what they need to know in terms of positioning, who's playing where, and so on. That's the key information the kids need to hear — not a long, overblown speech about "going out there and winning one for the Gipper."

You can pump them up for the game by having them do some rousing calisthenics or maybe some drills for which they're gleefully grunting and groaning. That's the kind of stuff kids love to do before a game to get psyched up. But in terms of that last second dramatic pep talk, well, that's not necessary.

When the game's over, don't waste your time trying to do a full-blown, postgame analysis with the team. Take no more than two minutes to talk with them, praise them for their efforts, and then send them on their way. You can talk to them about those parts of the game that need help in your next practice session.

Keep in Mind That Motivation Still Comes from within the Child

"My child shows great skills — speed, strength, and agility — but she really doesn't seem to want to practice much on her own. What can I do to motivate her to want to practice more?"

The most important part of motivation is that it has to come from within the child. No matter how much prodding, pushing, or threatening you do, unless the desire comes from within the youngster, words can't make them want to practice more.

What you can do is point out to the child what special or unique athletic gifts they have. Make the child aware that she has some special God-given abilities that she was born with. You can also help her develop a passion for sports when she's young and just starting out. Always let her look upon athletics as being fun — never as a chore or an obligation. Keep in mind that close to 80 percent of all kids quit playing organized sports by the time they reach the age of 13.

So let the child develop her own love for her sport. Especially when she's young, don't be so eager to push her to a higher level, to drill her on tougher or more demanding skills, or to make certain that she specializes in one sport.

Kids can and will motivate themselves — if they find the sport to be fun. If sports are fun for them, there's every chance that they will continue to play.

Be More Than Fair — Be a Good Coach

You have a real choice to make when you coach kids. On one hand, you can make every effort to ensure that these kids will remember playing on your team as a fun and positive experience. On the other, you can leave nightmarish memories with them that will gnaw at them and bother them for years to come.

Go to any group of adults today who are in their 30s or 40s, and you'll discover more than a few who can recall the hurtful or painful memories that they suffered when they played youth sports. Many adults can tell you about the time that "the coach played everybody in the game except me" or "the coach bawled me out in front of all my friends because I didn't catch a pop-up" and so on. What's noteworthy is that these disturbing events may have happened 20 or 25 years ago — but the adult bitterly recalls the incident as though it happened yesterday.

The way in which you treat the children is essential to their having fond memories of being on your team. Very few people can ever recall if their 5th grade youth basketball team or a 7th grade youth baseball team had a winning record — but nearly everyone can recall whether or not it was a fun experience. And if it was a fun experience, it was a direct result of the coach.

Remember That the Younger the Kids, the Less Important the Score

Don't worry about the scores of the games until the kids start worrying about it. That means, for the most part, kids aren't really going to be aware of which team is winning or losing until they're 9 or 10. If you're keeping league standings or taking notes on who was the leading scorer or other such statistics, bear in mind that they really don't have any meaning — especially for little kids.

While many coaches have a difficult time putting a loss behind them, children bounce back very quickly from a defeat — even a close defeat. If you struggle with losses, you may want to think twice about whether you should be coaching. Try to understand that winning and losing is definitely part of the game, but that you have to be able to learn to move beyond a loss. Do this by using defeats as learning experiences; that is, try to dissect those aspects of the team that need to be worked on and improved.

When in Doubt, Stand Back and Enjoy!

Sometimes, coaches become so absorbed in the Xs and Os of the sport, of trying to make certain that the kids put forward their best effort, and in putting everything into the team so that it does well, that they develop a kind of tunnel vision about the games. It's almost as though they're so focused on the game action that they have become immune to outside concerns or distractions.

Some coaches go so far as to instruct their spouses not to bother them on game day — when all of their attention is being centered on the upcoming contest. It isn't until after the game is over that these coaches can finally sit back and breathe again normally — assuming of course that the team won! This "win at all costs" mentality can quickly influence the kids as they begin to pick up on the coach's hyper-serious attitude and restrict themselves from being playful because they realize that this is all very serious business.

If you find yourself heading down this path, give yourself a timeout and take a step back. Coaching kids is strictly about having an enjoyable time, and about teaching kids the fundamentals of a game. Winning and losing are, of course, part of the game, especially as the children get older, but remember that as the coach, you set the tone for how the kids go about their game. And the kids who play for a fun-oriented coach always have a much better time than those who end up playing for a strict taskmaster.

As such, never take coaching kids more seriously than what it really is — otherwise, you'll miss all the fun!

Chapter 18

Ten (Actually, 20) Brief Tips for Becoming a Great Coach

*T*his chapter gives you a quick review of the key coaching tips given throughout this book, summarized in bite-sized nuggets. Chances are that you already know a lot of this from being around sports or from using parental common sense, so use this information as reminders when getting ready for the upcoming season. You can also use these tips as a kind of checklist to make sure you're on the right track.

Give Your Team Positive Experiences

This has to be your top priority, and you're going to have to work at it. But if you plan all of your practices and games and are sensitive to the individual needs of the kids on your team, everybody comes out a winner.

Organize a Pre-Season Team Meeting

This will be the most important meeting you'll have with your kids and their parents, and you have to make it mandatory. This meeting gives you the opportunity to meet the parents and their kids for the first time, to outline your policies and philosophies, and to make certain there are no misunderstandings for the coming season. This is especially important when discussing the concept of commitment — that is, not missing practices or games.

Know Your Team's Special Medical Needs

You need to know if a child has asthma, diabetes, or some other medical condition that may affect his health or play. You also need to be educated of what to do in case of an emergency.

Educate Yourself about the Sport

If you're going to coach, you have to know the rules!

Determine Your Coaching Style

Some coaches are lively and enthusiastic, others tend to smile and are quiet. Find what works for you. Just be careful not to become a yeller and screamer.

Set Realistic Expectations for the Kids

Not every kid is going to be a star, but all kids want to have fun. As the coach, you have to work with each child to help her progress and advance her individual skill level.

Be Sure Your Team Has the Proper Equipment

In most youth leagues, if a child isn't wearing the right equipment, the official won't even let him play. As the coach, it's your job to educate the kids and their parents about the importance of good equipment.

Organize Your Practice Sessions to Be Quick-Paced

The best practices are those in which the kids are moving from drill to drill, always on the go, and always progressing. By the end of the session, they feel as though they've truly accomplished their goals for the day.

Put Your Assistant Coaches to Work during Practices and Games

Too many head coaches become control freaks. That's silly. If you're lucky enough to have assistant coaches, utilize them. Delegate drills and tasks to them in a meaningful way. You'll be a better coach.

Remember That Parents Come to Games to Watch Their Own Kids Play

If you're the coach, you have to always remember this simple reality regarding youth sports. As such, make certain that every kid gets lots of quality playing time.

Keep a Detailed Scoresheet

This way, you know how much playing time each child on your team is getting, who's playing what position, and who has taken his or her turn sitting out of the game.

Use the Best Motivational Technique: Praise!

You can never go wrong if you use praise as a way to get the kids moving in the right direction.

Communicate, Communicate, Communicate

Oddly enough, too few coaches ever take the time to talk with the kids about skill development, strategies, sportsmanship, and so on. Talk to your young athletes as much as you can — they'll respond in a big way for you.

Teach Sportsmanship

And enforce it, too. Sportsmanship is a concept that has to be continually taught, enforced, and respected. As the coach, this task often falls on your shoulders.

Motivate by Walking Around

Spend some time each practice just walking around and addressing each child by her first name. Kids like it when the coach talks to them on a one-to-one basis.

Use Common Sense When Faced with Injuries

The child's physical health always comes first over the game. Be prepared for any medical emergency. Make certain you have a cell phone on hand just in case of any emergency.

Avoid a Post-Game Analysis at All Costs!

Give the kids a break right after the game. Save the post-game analysis of what happened in the game. Let the kids enjoy the moment, win or lose. You can work on improving their game at the next practice — not right after the game.

Give Upset Parents a Chance to Speak Their Piece

If a parent comes to you with a gripe or complaint, give him plenty of time to get his concerns off his chest. Don't try to even respond to them until he's had his moment. But after he's finished, give your explanations in a cordial and civil manner.

Remember That Travel Teams Can Also Mean Rejection

Lots of parents are eager to have their kids try out for a travel team. But if you're coaching a travel team, remind the parents ahead of time that while some kids will be chosen, many will be rejected. Dealing with a "rejected" child isn't easy for the parent or the coach.

Keep in Mind That Kids in Individual Sports Have Unique Pressures

And because they do, they often deal with disappointments and frustrations in a more personalized manner (see Chapter 5). You, as a coach, have to be sensitive to that.

Appendix A

Youth Sports Organizations

••

Multi-Sport Organizations

The Center for Sports Parenting
(This is my personal favorite, so I've listed it first.)
University of Rhode Island
P.O. Box 104
Kingston, RI 02881-0104
Phone: 800-447-9889
Web site: www.internationalsport.com

Amateur Athletics Union (AAU)
The Walt Disney World Resort
P.O. Box 10000
Lake Buena Vista, FL 32830-1000
Phone: 800-AAU-4USA
Web site: www.aausports.org

American Coaching Effectiveness Programs (ACEP)
P.O. Box 5076
Champaign, IL 61820
Phone: 217-351-5076

Boys and Girls Clubs of America
National Headquarters
1230 W. Peachtree St. NW
Atlanta, GA 30309
Phone: 404-815-5700
Web site: www.bgca.org

Disabled Sports USA
451 Hungerford Dr., Suite 100
Rockville, MD 20850
Phone: 301-217-0960
Web site: www.dsusa.org/dsusa.html

National Alliance for Youth Sports (NAYS)
2050 Vista Pkwy.
West Palm Beach, FL 33411
Phone: 561-684-1141
Web site: www.nays.org

National Association of Police Athletic Leagues (PAL)
618 US Highway 1, Suite 201
North Palm Beach, FL 33408
Phone: 561-844-1823

National Youth Sports Coaches Association (NYSCA)
2050 Vista Pkwy.
West Palm Beach, FL 33411
Phone: 800-729-2057; 561-684-1141
Web site: www.nays.org/nysca.html

National Youth Sports Safety Foundation, Inc.
333 Longwood Ave., Suite 202
Boston, MA 02115
Phone: 617-277-1171
Web site: www.nyssf.org

Special Olympics International Headquarters
1325 G St. NW, Suite 500
Washington, DC 20005-3104
Phone: 202-628-3630
Web site: www.specialolympics.org

YMCA of the USA
101 North Wacker Dr.
Chicago, IL 60606
Phone: 312-977-0031; 888-333-YMCA
Web site: www.ymca.net

Baseball and Softball Organizations

All American Amateur Baseball Association
331 Parkway Dr.
Zanesville, OH 43701
Phone: 614-453-8531

Amateur Athletics Union Baseball
The Walt Disney World Resort
P.O. Box 10000
Lake Buena Vista, FL 32830-1000
Phone: 800-AAU-4USA; 407-934-7200
Web site: www.aausports.org

Amateur Softball Association/USA Softball
2801 NE 50th St.
Oklahoma City, OK 73111
Phone: 405-424-5266
Web site: www.softball.org

American Amateur Baseball Congress
118-119 Redfield Plaza
P.O. Box 467
Marshall, MI 49068
Phone: 616-781-2002
Web site: www.voyager.net/aabc

American Legion Baseball
National Office
P.O. Box 1055
Indianapolis, IN 46206
Phone: 317-630-1213
Web site: www.legion.org/baseball

Babe Ruth Baseball & Softball
International Headquarters
1770 Brunswick Pike
Trenton, NJ 08638
Phone: 800-880-3142
Web site: www.baberuthleague.org

Baseball Canada/Canadian Federation of Amateur Baseball
1600 James Naismith Dr.
Gloucester, Ontario K1B 5N4
Phone: 613-748-5606
Web site: www.baseball.ca

Continental Amateur Baseball Association
82 University St.
Westerville, OH 43081
Phone: 614-899-2103

Dixie Baseball, Inc.
P.O. Box 877
Marshall, TX 75671-0877
Phone: 903-927-2255
Web site: www.dixie.org/main.html

Dizzy Dean Baseball
902 Highway 9 North
Eupora, MS 39744
Phone: 601-258-7626

Hap Dumont Baseball
P.O. Box 17455
Wichita, KS 67217
Phone: 316-721-1779

Little League Baseball, Inc.
P.O. Box 3485
Williamsport, PA 17701
Phone: 717-326-1074
Web site: www.littleleague.org

National Amateur Baseball Federation
P.O. Box 705
Bowie, MD 20718
Phone: 301-262-5005

PONY Baseball and Softball
P.O. Box 225
Washington, PA 15301
Phone: 724-225-1060
Web site: www.pony.org/hq/staff.html

Reviving Baseball in Inner Cities (RBI)
350 Park Ave.
New York, NY 10022
Phone: 212-339-7800

T-Ball USA Association
915 Broadway, Suite 1901
New York, NY 10022
Phone: 800-741-0845; 212-254-7911

USA Baseball/U.S. Baseball Federation
Hi Corbett Field
3400 East Camino Campestre
Tuscon, AZ 85716
Phone: 609-586-2381; 520-327-9700
Web site: www.usabaseball.com

Youth Baseball Athletic League
567 Alger Dr.
Palo Alto, CA 94306
Phone: 800-477-9225

Basketball Organizations

Amateur Athletics Union Boys Basketball
The Walt Disney World Resort
P.O. Box 10000
Lake Buena Vista, FL 32830-1000
Phone: 800-AAU-4USA; 407-934-7200

Amateur Athletic Union Girls Basketball
The Walt Disney World Resort
P.O. Box 10000
Lake Buena Vista, FL 32830-1000
Phone: 800-AAU-4USA; 407-934-7200

Basketball Canada
Phone: 613-748-5607
Web site: www.basketball.ca/

USA Basketball
5465 Mark Dabling Blvd.
Colorado Springs, CO 80918-3842
Phone: 719-590-4800
Web site: www.usabasketball.com/

Youth Basketball of America, Inc.
10325 Orangewood Blvd.
Orlando, FL 32821
Phone: 407-363-YBOA
Web site: www.yboa.org

Football Organizations

Football Canada/Canadian Amateur Football Association
Lansdowne Park / Civic Centre
1015 Bank St.
Ottawa, Ontario K1S 3W7
Phone: 613-748-5636

Pop Warner Little Scholars, Inc.
920 Town Center Dr.
Langhorne, PA 19047
Phone: 215-752-2691
Web site: www.dickbutkus.com/dbfn/popwarner/

United States Flag and Touch Football League
7709 Ohio St.
Mentor, OH 44060
Phone: 216-974-8735

Golf Organizations

American Junior Golf Association
2415 Steeplechase Ln.
Roswell, GA 30076
Phone: 770-998-4653
Web site: www.ajga.org/

Hook a Kid on Golf
National Alliance for Youth Sports
2050 Vista Pkwy.
West Palm Beach, FL 33411
Phone: 407-684-1141

Hockey Organizations

Canadian Hockey Association
Calgary Office
Father David Bauer Arena
2424 University Dr. NW
Calgary, Alberta T2N 3Y9
Phone: 403-777-3636

Ottawa Office
1600 James Naismith Dr.
Gloucester, Ontario K1B 5N4
Phone: 613-748-5613
Web site: www.canadianhockey.ca

Hockey North America/National Novice Hockey Association
Phone: 703-471-0400; 800-446-2539
Web site: www.hna.com

USA Hockey
1775 Bob Johnson Dr.
Colorado Springs, CO 80906
Phone: 719-576-USAH
Web site: www.usahockey.com

Youth Hockey Network
Web site: www.youthhockeynetwork.com

Soccer Organizations

American Youth Soccer Organization (AYSO)
12501 South Isis Ave.
Hawthorne, CA 90250
Phone: 310-643-6455; 800-USA-AYSO
Web site: www.soccer.org

Canadian Soccer Association
237 Metcalfe St.
Ottawa, Ontario K2P 1R2
Phone: 613-237-7678
Web site: www.canoe.ca/SoccerCanada/home.html

Soccer Association for Youth (SAY)
Phone: 513-769-3800; 800-233-7291
Web site: www.saysoccer.org/

Soccer in the Streets
149 South McDonough St., Suite 270
Jonesboro, GA 30236
Phone: 770-477-0354
Web site: www.sits.org

SuperClubs North America (USYSA)
Phone: 800-877-3790; 913-663-5425
Web site: www.upper90.com/

United States Amateur Soccer Association, Inc. (USASA)
Phone: 800-867-2945; 201-338-6153
Web site: www.usasa.com

United States Soccer Federation
1801-1811 South Prairie Ave.
Chicago, IL 60616
Web site: www.us-soccer.com

United States Youth Soccer Association, Inc.
899 Presidential Dr., Suite 117
Richardson, TX 75081
Phone: 800-4-SOCCER
Web site: www.usysa.org

Swimming Organizations

Swim America
2101 N. Andrews Ave. #107
Ft. Lauderdale, FL 33311
Phone: 800-356-2722
Web site: www.swimamerica.org

USA Swimming
One Olympic Plaza
Colorado Springs, CO 80909
Phone: 719-578-4578
Web site: www.usswim.org

Tennis Organizations

Arthur Ashe's National Junior Tennis League
P.O. Box 26129
San Francisco, CA 94126
Phone: 415-843-NJTL (6585)
Web site: www.geocities.com/~ashekids/

United States Professional Tennis Association
One USPTA Centre
3535 Briarpark Dr.
Houston, TX 77042
Phone: 713-97-USPTA
Web site: www.uspta.org

United States Tennis Association
White Plains, NY
Phone: 914-696-7000
Web site: www.usta.com

Track and Field Organizations

USA Track & Field
One RCA Dome, Suite 140
Indianapolis, IN 46225
Phone: 317-261-0500
Web site: www.usatf.org

Coaching Resources on the Web

The Center for Sports Parenting: A national clearinghouse of information for both coaches and sports parents. (This happens to be my favorite, so I've listed it first.)

Web site: www.internationalsport.com

Athletic Rules Study: This group sells computer software that helps increase your knowledge of the rules. Currently, they have versions for high school football, basketball, baseball, softball, and volleyball. All of their high school programs are approved by the National Federation of State High School Associations and are priced at $25.

Web site: www.rules-study.com/

The National Association for Sport and Physical Education: This group seeks to enhance knowledge and professional practice in sport and physical activity through scientific study and circulation of research to members and the public.

Web site: www.aahperd.org/naspe/naspe-main.html

The Positive Coaching Alliance: A not-for-profit organization based at Stanford University whose mission is to transform youth sports so sports can transform youth.

Web site: www.positivecoach.org

WeTeachSports: The mission of this group is to revolutionize the sporting lives of young and old, amateur and professional, individuals and teams by providing the best resources for communication, event organization, coaching, equipment, and motivational tools so that your time is spent coaching sports. They offer a full array of books, videos, and software for coaches, parents, and athletes.

Web site: www.weteachsports.com/

Youth Sports Instruction: This group furnishes helpful articles, a free newsletter, chat areas, and instructional products that will help parents and coaches teach children youth sports and sportsmanship.

Web site: www.youth-sports.com

Youth Sports Network: This site provides sporting event news, sports information, tools for coaching, player tips, sports statistics, health and fitness info, games, and more.

Web site: www.ysn.com

YouthSportsUSA: One of the most comprehensive youth sports sites on the Internet that also serves as a home on the Web of hundreds of sports leagues across the country.

Web site: www.youthsportsusa.com/

Appendix B

The Coach's Resource Kit

· ·

*T*his appendix is the place for first-time coaches to look for information and forms — from deciding whether to coach to putting together a scoresheet, this appendix is your coaching kit.

To Coach or Not to Coach

Take a few moments to go through the following checklist, just to make certain that you're well suited to coach kids. Bear in mind that most youth sports leagues are always looking for volunteers to help out, and chances are that your local youth sports group would love to have you get involved. But before you make that call to sign up, ask yourself the following:

- ✔ **Do you understand that kids are different from grown-ups?** Kids aren't miniature adults — they have different needs and attention spans than do adults. And different things are important to them on certain days: They may be more excited about getting uniforms, new shoes, or mitts than about competing or understanding a game plan. They'll probably be excited just to be on the team with other kids, doing something new. As the coach, you have to understand and accept this reality. If you can't, you may want to think twice about being their coach.

- ✔ **What age groups are you comfortable with?** Do you relate well to older kids? Are you scared of teenagers? Do you understand the intricate mind of 6- to 8-year-olds? Find out more about each age group in the "Developmental Phases of Young Athletes" section, later in this appendix.

- ✔ **How much time do you have?** Learning and coaching a sport requires a great time commitment that may be more than you think: You need to make up lineups for the games and meets, attend coaches meetings, schedule and attend parent meetings, take part in fundraising activities — and of course you still have to organize and run all the practice sessions.

- ✔ **Do you like to make or take telephone calls?** If you're going to coach, you will spend some significant time on the phone calling for directions, making certain the refs or officials are all set for the game, calling players about the weather, and so on. Plus, parents will be calling you to ask about their child's progress, problems, conflicts, and so on.

✔ **Do you like getting up early?** For some sports like swimming, tennis, ice hockey, and golf, you have to be comfortable with getting up at the crack of dawn because the time allocations of pools, rinks, courts, and courses are at a premium — you may have to arise in the dark and have special pre-dawn sessions.

✔ **Do you interact well with other adults?** As a coach of any age group, you have to work with the parents who can fight like tigers where their children are concerned. You also have to be engaging enough to attract assistant coaches who want to help you with practices and games.

✔ **Are you patient, calm, and able to laugh at yourself?** You'll need these attributes. All coaches need to have a solid sense of humor — you even have to be able to laugh at yourself and your own foibles from time to time.

✔ **Do you love the sport?** If you don't love (or learn to love) the sport, you may have difficulty stirring up enthusiasm; standing in the rain; dealing with officials, parents, other coaches; and raking fields, hauling equipment, and cleaning up game areas. In short, you may not love the sport, but if your child and his or her teammates do, do your best to try and learn to love it!

✔ **Will it be worth it?** Most coaches can't even measure how great the rewards are — you may have more fun that the kids do!

Developmental Phases of Young Athletes

It's a good idea just to review the physical and maturational stages of all kids as a measuring stick to remind that youngsters see the world — and especially sports — in different ways. What's presented below are broad generalizations, but they provide a chronology of athletic development. See Chapter 2 for further details.

Ages 1 to 3

By the time most children are 3 (keeping in mind that all kids develop their skills at their own pace!), they are discovering that the concept of "play" is a wonderfully self-satisfying activity. Bit by bit, more skills are developing, until around the age of 4 or 5 when their random play activities advance to the first beginnings of group games and sports.

Ages 4 to 8

The majority of kids at this age level are just happy to be wearing a shiny new uniform, to be a member of a team with their friends, and to be running around and having a good time. And you know what? That enthusiasm is really what you want your child to be learning at this stage because unless your youngster develops a true passion for his sport, he's not going to keep pursuing it as he gets older. In short, if it's fun, the child will keep on playing — ideally, right through middle school and into high school and maybe beyond.

- **Stay patient and open to the possibilities.** Give your child plenty of space and time to enjoy the experience of playing a variety of sports, and to try different approaches to their athletic activities. Allow her to gain the self-confidence that comes with trying and trying again.

- **Give praise.** Acknowledge the child's effort (not necessarily the outcome) as she struggles in her first attempts. Gentle but sincere praise and encouragement helps to ease her disappointment and wipe away her frustration, and will keep her pushing ahead to conquer that athletic skill.

- **Teach your child that doing her best is all that matters.** Winning or losing isn't something that a child can always control, but she can control what sort of effort she puts forth.

- **Let her have fun.** Give your little one the space she needs to try, fail, experiment, and ultimately, find her way. Let her laugh if she runs up to a soccer ball, takes a big swing with her leg, and falls on her fanny. Or if she hits a ball but then runs around the bases in the wrong direction. Or even if she's chatting with their friends on the bench and not really paying attention to what's going on in the game. Hey, at this tender age, that's all okay! Why? Because your kid is having fun!

✔ **Don't push.** Let kids play with kids their own age, and don't worry about summer camps or travel teams — all of this can wait until they're older. Overdoing a sport can lead to the child's burning out and walking away from it as young as 12 or 13.

✔ **If your child loses interest, find out why.** The reasons may range from a taunting teammate to a fear of injury, but when you uncover it, you can help your child find a solution.

Ages 9 to 12

By the time young athletes are 9 or 10, they're starting to exhibit the first real flashes of athletic mastery and ability. They're also beginning to show a cognitive understanding not only of the game, its rules, and some of its strategies, but also how those strategies can help them win instead of lose. And they enjoy being recognized as a youngster who shows some athletic talent and can perform a task well (for example, shooting a foul shot, kicking a soccer ball with either foot, being able to throw strikes over the plate, and so on).

This athletic development continues to build even more during ages 11 and 12. The flashes of athleticism become even more consistent in their appearance, and the youngster begins to get a handle on how to repeat these athletic skills over and over again.

✔ **Explain the rules.** As children reach the age of 9 or 10, along with their physical maturation comes a strong sense of fair play and "playing by the rules." It's as though they feel they are personally responsible for the outcome of the game, and to ensure a positive outcome, they have to "police" any perceived wrongdoings, especially when it comes to making calls on the field, rule interpretation, or any other potentially controversial situation. In effect, they'll start to challenge the grown-ups who are making the calls. It's important not to simply brush them off, but to take a few moments to explain the reasoning behind each call or move.

✔ **Let your child get emotional.** During these years, a loss or a disappointing performance may be accompanied by tears. Nothing can melt a parent's heart faster than to see your child's eyes well up with tear drops. What do you do? Be kind, sympathetic, and supportive. There's nothing wrong with your child crying because he feels that he didn't do well.

✔ **Teach and enforce sportsmanship.** Let him know (at an early age) that the issue of sportsmanship is not an issue to be taken lightly.

✔ **Help him acquire a sense of commitment.** But by the time they're 9, 10, and older, kids understand what it means to sign up for a team and, in effect, tell the coach (and the rest of the team) that they're going to be a solid member of the team. That means getting up early on rainy days and getting to practice on time, scheduling homework and other extracurricular obligations properly so that she doesn't have to miss a game, and calling the coach a few days ahead of a scheduling conflict to explain why she can't be at the practice or game that weekend.

Ages 13 and older

When the youngster reaches adolescence, many aspects of their athletic pursuits change dramatically. By the seventh and eighth grades, the youngsters who have both inherent athletic talent as well as a desire to improve their athletic skills continue to develop these abilities during this time. Cuts may be introduced in making a school-based team.

At the other end of the athletic spectrum, some kids, recognizing that perhaps their strengths lie somewhere other than sports, begin a process of self-evaluation (also called self-selection) about whether they want to continue competitively in sports, or perhaps find another extracurricular activity to pursue. Help your child understand, however, that staying physically fit is not just a convenience — it's an essential part of staying healthy for life.

High school sports bring a set of new priorities. For example, unlike the early years where winning should be nowhere near the top priority, at the high school varsity level, winning becomes a greater priority for the coach and the kids on the team. By this time in the student-athlete's career, he or she usually accepts that being victorious in a sporting event is what the team and the coach are shooting for. Nevertheless, the smart coach understands that the fun still resides in playing the game, not just for the top teenage athletes, but for as many of the team members as possible.

Parent Meeting Checksheet

Your initial meeting with parents should include the following topics. Chapter 7 gives you additional information.

✔ **Have all the essential information already typed out and ready to hand out.** Essential information includes your name and home phone number, as well as the assistant coaches' names and numbers.

✔ **Find out who can help you.** If you haven't found a team parent yet (a team parent helps out with making phone calls in case of bad weather, getting travel directions, bringing juice/water to games, and so on), this is the perfect time to ask for a volunteer.

✔ **Explain the league rules of participation.** Let all the parents know if there are any mandatory rules regarding how much of each game every child must play.

✔ **Explain the league rules regarding equipment and safety instructions.** This may take a few minutes, but you want to address this important topic in this first meeting.

✔ **Ask the parents to review with you any medical concerns regarding their children in a private conversation, perhaps even after the meeting.** Medical information is just as important as the safety equipment issue! Because many parents would prefer to discuss this personal matter with you in confidence rather than in public, give them that option. Be sure to get information about any lingering or healing injuries that a child on the team may have.

✔ **Discuss candidly with the moms and dads what you expect from them, especially with regard to their conduct at practices and games.** Naturally, you expect them to behave as mature adults and as positive role models in good sportsmanship for the kids. Reinforce that expectation.

✔ **Talk about sportsmanship and how you expect the kids to behave.** Using examples, explain to the kids what it means to play in a sportsmanlike manner (shaking hands with opponents after the game, treating the officials with respect, no trash talking or taunting, and so on).

✔ **Go over team discipline briefly.** This tends to be something of a broad topic, and you don't want to get bogged down here or give the kids a long list of disciplinary rules. For the time being, just tell the kids and their parents that you expect them to be on time, come to the practices, and if they can't make it to a practice or game for any reason, to contact you via telephone — ideally at least 24 hours ahead of time.

✔ **At the end of the meeting, take a few moments to hand out schedules, directions to away games, and uniforms. (Make sure that the kids try them on and that they fit before they leave!)** In addition, take some time to meet and greet the parents you don't know. Try to learn each child's first name and introduce yourself to each one.

First-Practice Checksheet

The most important aspect of running a practice is preparing for it so that you're organized when you get there! The truth is, the easy — and fun — part of running a practice is following your script during the practice session. If you've done your homework in the week before practice and have followed the list below, practice sessions will be something to look forward to.

- ✔ **Line up an assistant or two** — or three, as you can never have too many — and meet with them before your first practice so that he or she can better understand your philosophy and style. You'll also to be able to let them know where you'll need help.

- ✔ **Arrange (with the help of your assistants) the non-sporting but essential stuff:** organizing rides, making up the roster, putting together refreshment lists for parents, organizing team fundraising activities, collecting and distributing uniforms, and determining a method for keeping stats.

- ✔ **Create a plan for your first practice:**

  - **Introducing yourself and your assistant(s):** Explain the roles of each.

  - **Meeting the team:** Ask the team members to introduce themselves, and try to place the faces with the names.

  - **Filling out player information cards and the team roster:** See the two following sections for examples.

  - **Presenting the team rules**

  - **Determining who has what experience:** Find out how many have played the sport before. Find out whether each athlete likes the sport: If a child doesn't want to be there, consider scheduling a meeting with the parent.

  - **Explaining and establishing the practice routine:** Follow approximately the same format every session.

  - **Warming up**

  - **Breaking the team into small groups and testing skill levels:** In addition to physical skills, see how they react with each other. See who is aggressive, who is passive. Give individuals in the group specific instructions. See how they respond. Do you have to tell them twice? Do they forget the instruction? Are they easily distracted? Take notes.

    Rotate a few drills so that everyone gets a chance to practice different skills. Allow them some time to mix and get to know each other between sets.

  - **Keeping the first practice short:** Give them something to work on at home before the next practice.

  - **Meeting as many of the parents as you can at the first practice.**

Player Information Card

It may seem like busy work, but these individualized player information cards come in handy throughout the season. Always carry the *complete* collection of them to every game and practice.

Name: Position(s) or event(s):

Address: Phone:

Parent's name(s):   Work number(s):

Cell phone or pager number(s):   Emergency contact:

Medical precautions:

Doctor's name: Doctor's phone number:

T-shirt size: XS S M L XL   Shorts size: XS S M L XL

Shoe size: Uniform number:

Other key information:

Roster

Every team needs a roster. If your league doesn't provide you with one or they give you a roster of names and numbers that's hard to follow, put together your own roster. Here's a sample to follow.

Make enough copies of your roster to give out to every player on your team.

Head coach: _____   Phone: _____

Assistant coach: _____   Phone: _____

Assistant coach: _____   Phone: _____

Our practice time is every Saturday morning from 8:00 to 9:15 on Field B at Town Park.

Roster of the Armonk Armadillos, Division II Girls 3-G

Player name	Age	Address	Parent name	Phone

Scoresheet

Your scoresheet is an essential part of your coaching responsibility. Simply list all of the players on your team, and with each period of the game, mark down what position they played or if they sat out. Also mark the team you played, the date, and any special comments or notes about a particular player in the game (for example, was one of your players ill or did one of your kids miss the game?).

The following chart is for a soccer team. Note that there are 15 girls on the roster and only 11 can play at one time. I keep track of each child's position on the field by using a simple abbreviation for the basic positions: G = goal-keeper, D = defense, M = midfielder, and F = forward. Depending on the sport you're coaching, try to develop a similar system of short abbreviations so that you can quickly track which kids played which position during the game, and which kids sat out.

In this example, I rotate the players through different positions and no player is ever forced to sit out twice. In other words, everybody has to take their turns sitting out before one child is asked to sit out twice.

Whatever you do, don't lose or throw away your scoresheets! You need to keep them for the entire season, just in case a parent or a player contends that they weren't given enough playing time or weren't allowed to play their favorite position.

June 10, 2000	Armonk Armadillos v. Armonk Anteaters			
Name	**1st quarter**	**2nd quarter**	**3rd quarter**	**4th quarter**
Alyssa	F	XX	D	M
Samantha	G	XX	F	M
Patty	M	XX	D	F
Jane	M	D	XX	G
Margy	—	—		—
Amy	D	F	XX	M
Lindsay	D	F	XX	M
Michelle	XX	M	F	D
Ashley	F	D	M	XX

June 10, 2000

Name	1st quarter	2nd quarter	3rd quarter	4th quarter
Stefanie	XX	M	D	F
Emily	F	D	M	XX
Grace	D	G	M	XX
Karyn	D	M	F	D
Nicole	M	M	G	D
Sharon	M	F	M	F

Game notes: Margy was not at the game because she was ill. Karyn, Nicole, and Sharon all played the entire game. They'll be the first players to sit out in next week's game.

Bill of Rights for Young Athletes

- The right to participate in sports.
- The right to participate at a level commensurate with each child's developmental level.
- The right to have qualified adult leadership as their coach.
- The right to participate in safe and healthy environments.
- The right of children to share in the leadership and decision-making of their sport participation.
- The right to play as a child and not as an adult.
- The right to proper preparation for participation in sports.
- The right to an equal opportunity to strive for success.
- The right to be treated with dignity.
- The right to have fun in sports.

Reprinted from Guidelines for Children's Sports *(1979) with permission from the National Association for Sport and Physical Education (NASPE), 1900 Association Drive, Reston, VA 20191.*

Bill of Rights for Coaches of Young Athletes

- The right to expect young athletes to attend and play hard during all practices and games.
- The right to have young athletes follow the rules of the team and the league.
- The right to organize appropriate practices, without disruption from young athletes or their parents.
- The right to make coaching mistakes and to learn from them.
- The right to expect good sportsmanship from young athletes and their parents.
- The right to be treated with dignity by young athletes and their parents.

Index

Notes

Notes

Notes

Notes

Notes

Notes

Notes

Notes

Notes

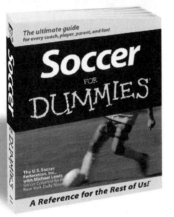

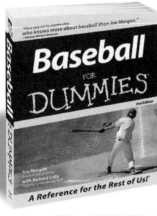

Discover Dummies Online!

The Dummies Web Site is your fun and friendly online resource for the latest information about *For Dummies* books and your favorite topics. The Web site is the place to communicate with us, exchange ideas with other *For Dummies* readers, chat with authors, and have fun!

Ten Fun and Useful Things You Can Do at www.dummies.com

1. Win free *For Dummies* books and more!
2. Register your book and be entered in a prize drawing.
3. Meet your favorite authors through the IDG Books Worldwide Author Chat Series.
4. Exchange helpful information with other *For Dummies* readers.
5. Discover other great *For Dummies* books you must have!
6. Purchase Dummieswear® exclusively from our Web site.
7. Buy *For Dummies* books online.
8. Talk to us. Make comments, ask questions, get answers!
9. Download free software.
10. Find additional useful resources from authors.

Link directly to these ten fun and useful things at
http://www.dummies.com/10useful

For other technology titles from IDG Books Worldwide, go to
www.idgbooks.com

Not on the Web yet? It's easy to get started with *Dummies 101®: The Internet For Windows® 98* or *The Internet For Dummies®* at local retailers everywhere.

Find other *For Dummies* books on these topics:
Business • Career • Databases • Food & Beverage • Games • Gardening • Graphics • Hardware
Health & Fitness • Internet and the World Wide Web • Networking • Office Suites
Operating Systems • Personal Finance • Pets • Programming • Recreation • Sports
Spreadsheets • Teacher Resources • Test Prep • Word Processing

IDG BOOKS WORLDWIDE BOOK REGISTRATION

Register This Book and Win!

We want to hear from you!

Visit **http://my2cents.dummies.com** to register this book and tell us how you liked it!

✔ Get entered in our monthly prize giveaway.

✔ Give us feedback about this book — tell us what you like best, what you like least, or maybe what you'd like to ask the author and us to change!

✔ Let us know any other *For Dummies*® topics that interest you.

Your feedback helps us determine what books to publish, tells us what coverage to add as we revise our books, and lets us know whether we're meeting your needs as a *For Dummies* reader. You're our most valuable resource, and what you have to say is important to us!

Not on the Web yet? It's easy to get started with *Dummies 101*®: *The Internet For Windows*® *98* or *The Internet For Dummies*® at local retailers everywhere.

Or let us know what you think by sending us a letter at the following address:

For Dummies Book Registration
Dummies Press
10475 Crosspoint Blvd.
Indianapolis, IN 46256

...FOR DUMMIES ™

BESTSELLING BOOK SERIES